Endorsements

"A compelling, heart warming book, gracefully and beautifully written. Luminous wisdom unfolds page after page and the author's courage and resilience shines forth for all of us."

John Bradshaw, theologian, host of nationally televised PBS series and best selling author.

"This is "wisdom literature." It is fresh, faith filled, and written with contemporary images. What hope it will give you to know there are people like Patricia Forbes out there! Read, and walk through a widely opened door."

Fr. Richard Rohr, O.F.M.
Center for Action and Contemplation
Albuquerque, New Mexico

"A magnificent book! Patricia Forbes paints word pictures into which we can step, giving new meaning to emotions we all experience. With a unique and vivid artistry, she connects the path from everyday events to profound truth. She sees universal meanings in the ordinary and opens doors for all of us."

Robert R. Ball, theologian, author, teacher and lecturer

"Patricia graciously invites us into her inner most sanctum of consciousness—that very private spot where many of us hide our pain, fears, and confusion. Her stories are our stories. The author paves the way for us from darkness to light. Her courageous and determined journey will leave you with inspirational stepping stones of creative thought lighting the way to our own Open Door.

Gerald Slaton, LCSW

"These healing stories open our heart, minds and our souls with their reflections. Each chapter brings comfort, wisdom and inspiration. The author crafts her words and thoughts into gems. She opens herself in order to help others heal their grief, better understand their relationships, navigate change and ultimately to live with intention. This author wanted to leave the legacy of her journey for her children and grandchildren. She did so much more!"

Judith G. Dowling, Psy.D., Clinical Psychologist

THE OPEN DOOR

THE OPEN DOOR

◆

Meditations on Living
an Authentic Life

PATRICIA FORBES

iUniverse, Inc.
New York Lincoln Shanghai

THE OPEN DOOR
Meditations on Living an Authentic Life

iUniverse, Inc.

For information address:
iUniverse, Inc.
2021 Pine Lake Road, Suite 100
Lincoln, NE 68512
www.iuniverse.com

ISBN: 0-595-32870-9

Printed in the United States of America

This book is dedicated with love to my children, Jeanine and Carver, who loyally traveled the road beside me, and to my precious grandchildren, Allen, Patricia, Elizabeth, and Martha Elster, Cameron and Paige Jones. And to my big brother, Arthur Lee Forbes, who unfailingly offered me his hand. While your journeys may at times be stalled and you may have questions that seem unanswerable, it is my hope that you may be led through your own *Open Door* and into the sunshine.

This book is also written in memory of my beloved ones, Janis and Lee, whose gentle spirits remain deep within my soul.

Contents

Acknowledgments

These vignettes would not have been put in book form without the firm urging of friends and family who steadfastly rallied my at times flagging spirits and daily applauded my efforts. Those whose consistent interest and support include Judith Dowling, Bobbi Owens, Sib Ellis, Kyle Reno, Jane and Bill Gibson, and members of the Giacomini family. I am grateful also to my three nieces, Corinne, Tricia, and Dana for their loving approval and encouragement. I am thankful to Gerald Slaton, who walked me through the paths of grief recovery.

A special word of thanks goes to my loyal cheerleader editor, Judy Logan. Without her assurance, advocacy, and efforts, my writing would not have evolved into a book.

To my spiritual teacher, Father Richard Rohr, I give my deep gratitude. Franciscan priest Richard Rohr is founder of the Center for Action and Contemplation in Albuquerque, New Mexico. He gives retreats and lectures internationally.

Father Richard, your books and tapes strengthened my belief and taught me how to listen to my heart. Your words echoed deep within and opened me to experience more of the blessings of faith.

I also offer gratitude to Father Vince Hovley of Sacred Heart Retreat House in Sedalia, Colorado, for the inspirational and beautiful photography that he so graciously allowed me to use for this memoir.

Preface

The most valuable legacy I can leave my loved ones is my journey. This book is an effort to convey to my children and grandchildren my path, both the light stories as well as the deeper shadows that life presents. My wish is to simply talk about the steps I chose which led me to the open door through which I walked—in spite of fear and unknowing—into a place of peace and comfort.

Every now and then there are opportunities to pass from our known world into an unknown world, to attend the birth of a new self. In order to experience this birth, we have to step through the doorway. But we are not ready until we are ready.

For the first half of my life, I was not ready. Instead, I was propelled along the current with my contemporaries, more or less falling into doorways rather than choosing them. Whatever path friends took, whatever path looked promising I took.

Through the years, however, building slowly inside was a shift in perception, and this silent movement—long in process—pushed one day into full consciousness, calling for profound and deliberate changes in how I lived my life. One day the spring simply bubbled to the surface and there was nothing I could do but welcome it. It was either accept this new way or die a slow inner death. Unlike the salmon, I had to turn and swim upstream to live.

The depth of this knowing astounds me now. I simply awakened one morning and knew that today was the day to stand by the truth that had been so long germinating inside. It was time to let go of worn out ideas and beliefs. Like a trapeze artist, in order to grasp the bar swinging towards me I had to let go of the old bar, the bar I was terrified to release. There was no question as to whether I could continue playing by the rules I'd gone along with for years, the script I'd accepted for my life. For the first time, opinions of those around me did not enter into the equation. I knew that once I began this journey there would be much confusion and strong effort to draw me back into old patterns. But I knew with quiet certitude that my life was evolving the only way that it could. And no matter how it all turned out, it would be all right.

There is a subtle atmospheric beat in the world that some people follow all their lives—the norm, the expected cultural sanctions that give the green light to actions. For some, this precise beat is comfortable and works for their lifetime. But for others, there might come a time when that beat becomes constricting. I felt out of balance, as though I'd been walking with one foot on the curb and one foot in the street.

Years after this upheaval, I read a poem whose message thrust itself into my heart—"The Journey," by Mary Oliver. Graphically, it described what happened to me.

The Journey

One day you finally knew
what you had to do, and began,
though the voices around you
kept shouting
their bad advice—
though the whole house
began to tremble
and you felt the old tug
at your ankles.
"Mend my life!"
each voice cried.
But you didn't stop
you knew what you had to do,
though the wind pried
with its stiff fingers
at the very foundations,
though their melancholy

was terrible.
It was already late
enough, and a wild night.
and the road full of fallen
branches and stones.
But little by little
as you left their voices behind,
the stars began to burn
through the sheets of clouds,
and there was a new voice
which you slowly
recognized as your own,
that kept you company
as you strode deeper and deeper
into the world,
determined to do
the only thing you could do—
determined to save
the only life that you could

Mary Oliver

Looking back, I saw that I had become lost in anxiety and worry over others, lost in trying to fix things for them, a circle of repeated patterns slowly tightening around me. Roger Housden in his elegant book, *Ten Poems to Change Your Life*, says in his interpretation of Mary Oliver's poem:

> To walk on despite all the pleas for you to come back is to know that you are free from the clutches of guilt. When you are free of the grip of guilt and fear, love blooms—love of the truth. You will say what you have to say, and do what you have to do; not out of anger nor irresponsibility, but because if you do not cling to the truth, you know you will die. What we die to is an outworn way of being in the world. The directness of this knowing, quiet yet strong can propel you out of your habitual perceptions of life and into the unknown before you have even a moment to think twice about it.[1]

In his tape, *Sermon on the Mount: Awakening of the Heart,* my spiritual mentor, Father Richard Rohr, says,

> All you can do is be ready. It's about awakening the eyes, the ears, the heart, and asking God to ready your heart. And when the door shows itself, pray to have the eyes to recognize the door, and the courage to walk through it.[2]

After many years of marriage, my husband and I found ourselves drifting in different directions—speaking different languages, which stretched the fabric of our marriage. Try as we might, we seemed unsuccessful in connecting these paths. This diversion deserves no finger of blame. It was no ones fault. The catalyst to the moment of truth for me was the plight of our youngest child. She had a serious, chronic mental illness about which her father and I could not come to agreement concerning treatment. I was leaning heavily upon professionals. He was not. As so often happens in a family, a serious, chronic illness of a member brings the family tighter together or it splits it apart. Somehow we could not talk about her illness. We sought counseling and I thought we reached a consensus only to have denial tighten its grip and mute the painful words between us. Finally, this rift became an immovable obstacle and the bridge once between us became a concrete roadblock that ended our walk together. After graduating from college, our son developed bi-polar illness, but his dad and I were largely unaware for some time of the severity of his condition as he protected us from knowing, and as an adult he was in charge of his own life. But when we did learn about his condition, it appeared that we weren't on the same page about this either.

The morning came when I just knew that the time was now—today was the day. The marriage ended. There was nothing else I could do. And when I stepped through that door, frightening as it was, I knew it

---

1. Roger Housden, *Ten Poems to Change Your Life* (Harmony Books, 2001), P. 14.
2. Richard Rohr, O.F.M., Sermon *on the Mount: Awakening of the Heart* (Cincinnati, Ohio, Saint Anthony Messenger Press, 1992, series of eight tapes)

was right. Three years later I moved west, back to my beloved mountains.

Events and tragedies that appeared down the road only strengthened my walk. After only six years of a fulfilling second marriage, I lost this husband to heart disease. Three years later, my son took his life as the result of his illness, and three years after that I lost my daughter in the same catastrophic way because of the ravages of her mental illness. These were the years before medical science arrived with often-successful medication. My losses broke my heart, wounded my spirit, and cracked open the earth I stood upon. But my faith upheld me, and the door I'd stepped through offered a continuity and strength that drew me further along my path. There was nothing else to do but follow.

After the long path of grief receded, allowing me to see ahead again, I experienced a new flow to life, like a cleaned out artery. Now there seemed to be a fresh balance. I was moving in a direction that felt natural. I trusted in the unseen, in the sustaining power of God whom I intuitively reached for. There was a new voice I slowly recognized as my own, that kept me company as I strode deeper and deeper into the world, determined to do the only thing I could do, determined to save the only life that I could.

The following essays hold the lessons, which carried me forward in good stead, gave me the wisdom to handle whatever life handed me.

1

Survival Tool Kit

The Most Important Thing I Learned

I learned a lot while growing up. First I learned the basics, like how to braid my hair, ride a bike, and cook spaghetti. Then how to solve math problems, to make and keep friends, to be helpful to others. Next came how to drive a car, graduate from college, interview for a job, and work full time. And of course I learned how to choose a mate, get married, and have children.

I mastered juggling responsibilities, directed the building of a house, and in any spare time I read books and more books. I spent time selecting and filling our home with beautiful things. I became able to organize family life with four children, run a complicated chauffeuring service to three different schools, and support my husband in his career.

I filled every nook and cranny of life with activities and talk—lots and lots of everything available and imaginable, providing it was affordable. I learned how to arrange flowers, knit, and volunteer at the hospital. Everything was full, full, full, like a spinning birthday piñata.

Now, later in life, I've learned an invaluable fact, at least for me. Fulfillment isn't in the gathering of possessions, the accumulation of prestige, or gathering information. The good life isn't measured for me in quantity. The good life comes with letting go. Emancipating grown children. Letting go of responsibility and control. Releasing toxic people. Weeding out the unnecessary. Freedom comes in saying, "No." It comes with the humility of saying, "I don't know."

I'd thought happiness could be figured out in my head following a fixed formula, but I was wrong. Happiness is moveable, flexible, and appears with generous portions of acceptance of what life presents.

Squirrel Courage

I watched a squirrel this morning on my walk. The city is re-paving the road through the three-mile park, and big machines rumble down the path, moving old pavement.

This particular squirrel was preparing to cross the road. He halted at the edge, alert for danger. His tail was curved in a question mark. "Shall I cross now? Is there one of those huge machines coming? Any bicycles racing down the path? Can I cross safely?" I could imagine these questions etched in his posture. Satisfied, he entered the danger zone and sprinted across the road.

It seemed the squirrel was imbued with innate wisdom. He paused at the road and took in the signals, gathering information before advancing. Often I find myself on impulse movement—doing something immediately without first checking not only the outside environment but also my inner awareness. Having granted the inner signals to come through, I often find my first impulse would have been in error.

There is a saying in the book that guides Twelve Step programs, "Pause when agitated," that has served me well. Since I started paying attention to these three words, I have an increased possibility of choosing outcomes of events. I paid more attention to the sentence someone once said, "When we choose an action we also choose a consequence."

For most of my life, not trusting myself, I have given credence to others before myself. Looking back I can see that my body tried to guide me, give me its advice. I feel tension in my stomach; something hurts inside; I feel uncomfortable. I need to pay attention to these body signals. If I pause, like the squirrel, and wait a moment before taking action, I find a true path to follow, one that feels good and opens up naturally.

If I'm struggling, usually I'm on the wrong path. Not necessarily the wrong path for someone else, but one that doesn't fit for me in that particular circumstance.

Thank you, little squirrel, for the simple lesson this morning, one of the many that awareness brings, and they come in the simple, the daily, the small events. It is an exciting adventure to look daily for the "teacher," which today was a squirrel.

Ancient Wisdom

I sit this morning under a one-hundred-year-old tree in the park. The lowest branches dip down to meet the ground, the leaves tickling the grass as they move in the breeze. It's like a hideaway I remember from childhood. I am hidden, protected from other park visitors.

If I were to sit here, fixed in time, these dipping leaves would turn golden brown and fall to the ground. Wind would soar and abate. In due time bare gray branches and limbs would be neatly layered in white. Snow would fall.

The grooving of the ancient bark reveals the wisdom of one hundred years. I look up. Aged branches do not rise in a straight line. Like life, they bend and turn and twist, branching off in new directions. And like human beings, each tree is individual in its branching. I am aware of the presence of God in this, my secret hiding place. I feel the wisdom that reaches out from the base of this tree to the heavens above. I feel the permanence, being rooted, and the security this solid tree represents. How many stories and secrets this ancient tree must know—a trusted friend whose silence is guaranteed.

The bark has absorbed years of laughter; its branches have presided over the banquets of picnics, provided shelter from storms, and observed the hugs of human love. Under these thick, old, veined branches, tears of broken dreams have been shed, stolen moments of love shared, arguments resolved.

I feel trust here. Trust in an ancient wisdom long nurtured by sun and rain. I taste serenity and mystery here. It is as if this ancient tree is an old friend who says to me, "Rest and let go. Let it be. Everything is all right."

Fixed Model

I used to love to watch my older brother put together model airplanes. When the gluing and fixing was finished, we'd go to a vacant lot and watch the model sail into the sky. What a thrill! We enjoyed many such carefree moments together growing up.

Then life intruded. I grew up and tried to place the fixed pieces of my childhood into the larger outline of life. I became surprised, then disbelieving, then frustrated when life presented such a different picture than my childhood. "But the model in my brain of how life should be is so much better," I protested. "I'm sorry," life said, "but this is your curriculum, and learning what to put aside will be your greatest task."

The halls of higher education inscribed the words for me on marble walls: "The Truth Shall Set You free." I learned the truth that I could not have a fixed model about how anything would be.

I observed that my anger surfaced most often because the circumstance or person I faced at that time refused to fit my model of how they should be. My expectations became resentments waiting to happen. And I found that quite often, if not all the time, my own mind was my adversary. Its clinging to old ideas and plans was precisely what caused me pain. I had to let go of these dated ideas. They no longer served me.

What a task! To let go and just glide in the now. The childhood airplane now served as the model. I couldn't plan exactly where the wind would take my plane, couldn't organize its path through the sky, couldn't foresee where it would land. The truth is that each flight is a first. I can set it up, get everything ready, but once flight takes place, I have to relinquish expectations and accept its path as being the correct path for that day.

Tomorrow is another day, another plan, another take off, and another landing.

Anchor

In the movie, *Girl Interrupted,* adapted from the book by Susanna Dayson,[1] the head nurse in a psychiatric hospital is talking to a young woman who is not progressing to expectation. The nurse instinctively knows this girl could move on with her life if she chooses. The nurse puts a protective hand on the girl's shoulder and says, "Don't drop anchor here."

That sentence echoes inside me. It's so expressively simple. How often have I dropped anchor right where I am when I've traveled but halfway. I can think of many occasions when I've thought the race was finished when it was just beginning, the many times I've quit just before the finish line.

I play tennis, and many times I've been reminded by better players to follow through. It seems I hit the ball squarely in the center of my racket, but the ball goes into the net because my hand does not follow the stroke through. The beginning of my stroke is on target, but the finish is lame and the ball goes awry.

Many times lack of confidence is the net that catches the ball in mid-flight. A high school gym teacher took me aside one day and said, "It's very sad for me to watch you. You have perfect balance and good timing and great eye contact, but over and again you do not try. Believe in yourself!" She was right. For some reason, I expected very little of myself. I dropped anchor on the thought that I could not win if I competed.

Many times we drop anchor on the job, thinking this is as far as we can go. We reach a comfort level and fear stretching beyond it. The greatest example of pushing beyond is the Biblical Abraham. Set up comfortably, he had his family and a full life when God told him to leave everything and everyone behind and follow Him. Abraham,

---

1.   Susanna Dayson, *Girl Interrupted* (New York, Vintage Books, A Division of Random House, Inc., 1993)

without doubt or question, obeyed the call to move on. This required not only faith but also belief in self.

The anchor of our ship of life can be dropped at any time, but there is a wide open sea to explore, and when we think, "This is as good as it's going to get," just around the bend of tomorrow there might be something even more interesting, more beautiful awaiting us.

Off the Stage

In young adulthood, I thought the object of a satisfying life was to be in complete charge of one's life. This was as it should be—everyone the star of his own play.

And I positioned myself just so, center stage. Thing is, there were all these other people on my stage with whom I had to interact. I wanted to place them as I saw fit, position everybody around the center, which was me. This much I know: my plan did not work.

I became angry, hurt, put off and put out by others' actions on *my* stage. They just wouldn't follow directions. These "others" had their own ideas of the play to be held on my stage. They strutted and pulled out of line and generally did nothing to contribute to the play that I held in my hand. They said the wrong things at the wrong time, and the play went flying wildly along uncharted waters.

Finally I yielded to the fact that my play was not my play; it was simply one of many plays being acted out on the stage of life. I got it that I could step off the stage, just get off, and let the *big* director, God, direct the play as he saw fit.

This was a big hurdle, and one I thought I'd finally mastered. However, I notice that I still have the desire to drag my director's chair onto other stages, my best friend's stage, or my grown children's stages. I, with wisdom born of heartache, see exactly how the play should proceed in other people's lives. I imagine the scenes: I've written the words and actions for them, always with happy endings.

But again I discover the play has a life of its own, despite my careful planning. Scenes laid out so precisely on paper melt down, become something quite different. Words and actions have a spontaneous force in which I have no connection; they have a life of their own and proceed without prompting.

Somewhere along the way, it came to me with a "Hello!" that the plays of my friends and family, as well as my own, are exactly as they should be, regardless of the change of scene or dialogue from the one that I, with good intentions, created. They become fascinating to watch. I get off the stage. I sit in the audience and watch with admiration and some anxiety as the plays for these treasured friends and family unfold in their own time, exactly as they are designed by God, each play tailored to the person for specific life lessons to be learned. Sometimes these lessons have to be repeated many times before they are learned, and sometimes they are ignored and never learned. But no longer the director, I can only watch—and perhaps say a little prayer.

So I repeat to myself, "Let go. Stay in the audience. You do not have responsibility for the beginning, the middle, or the end of this play. You are not in charge."

The Dye of the World

Father Vince Hovley at Sacred Heart Retreat House in Sedalia, Colorado, says that the color of our thoughts dyes our soul. And the color of our soul dyes our world.

For me, that indicates the individuality of how we see things, that even though we look upon the same scene, often we have totally different responses.

Yesterday, while taking a walk in the park with a neighbor, we saw an elderly man and woman walking together. We'd been discussing the difficulties people have in seeing things alike, being on the same wavelength. When I observed this couple, my thought was, "What a nice afternoon to be walking with your husband." I expected any moment he would take her hand. My neighbor's observation was different. Rather than seeing a married couple, she saw conflict, a woman dressed for a date, a skirt visible under her woolen coat. The man had on a baseball jacket. My neighbor's thoughts were, "She's all ready to go dancing, and he's going to the ball game." Same sight, different perceptions.

On another occasion, I was voicing to a friend an idea that my therapist friend, Gerald, had—that everyone should have a mental board of directors to consult when problems occur. I pictured the different suggestions these people would offer in their solutions. I told her just who would be on my board: Amelia Earhart, the two men occasionally appearing on television programs during times of world stress—one a priest, the other a rabbi—referred to as the "God Squad," Gerald—and also, Ralph Waldo Emerson, J.D. Salinger, and Clint Eastwood—to name just a few.

My friend stopped me, "Clint Eastwood? Why on earth, Clint Eastwood?" Later on that morning, she again said, "I can't believe you have Clint Eastwood on your board!"

I laughed. You can have Mickey Mouse on your board if you want. I like the quiet unflappability, the easiness of Clint and he *is* on my mental board. The things I register may be totally different from yours. Not better, not worse, just different.

I have no doubt that the pictures I paint in my head, my every thought, color my worldview. And the actions that result from these thoughts do dye the world in which I live, like a splash of ink in a tub of water.

I am uncomfortable with what I perceive to be the loud and brash, whereas another may see and hear this behavior as excitement and challenge. I color my world with what I hear, see, and feel.

The coloring changes from time to time. On a day when I feel blue, my landscape is muted, and my actions that day reveal this. When things in my private world are going well, the color of my world is brighter.

A negative, constant color of gray or black will surely produce a dark dye both within our inner climate and how we look at our world.

Awareness of Vince Hovley's simple statement strikes me as a valid check on how our thoughts affect our personal world.

I Don't Know

It must have taken all of my youth into adulthood for me to say, "I don't know," out loud.

My father was vice president of an energy company that was expanding in which he was totally involved. My father was an intelligent man who had the ability to charm as well as lead. I loved his sense of humor and the positive, charismatic energy he exuded. He had answers to everything. Unfortunately, I grew up believing that my need to ask questions emitted a faint aroma of shame.

It was not until my forties that I was relieved of the shame of not having answers. I found my own voice, dropped my facade of knowledge, let in the presence of humility, and learned to ask for information.

Words developed new meanings. What I previously thought of as weakness—not having answers—turned out to be one of the strengths that liberated me. What freedom when I could honestly say, "I don't know." I felt like I'd been an actress pretending to be something I wasn't on a daily basis. When I finally walked off the "stage of answers," it felt right, it felt good, like truth.

In hindsight, I see that perhaps I could have done things better, been more helpful to loved ones if I'd had the humility and honesty to say out loud, without fear, these three words, "I don't know."

In the old days, instead of handling problems by taking time, thinking things through, I could quickly fire off a solution to any problem presented. I used my intuition and imagination and came up with immediate answers, some right on target, some totally wrong, and some solutions that added more questions. But there was certainly nothing slow about my response. As one friend said of me, "She is out the door, down the street, and around the corner before we rise from our chairs." At the time, I thought this was a compliment. Now I'm not so sure. I notice that my daughter, Jeanine, rearing her four children, instinctively knows how to say, "I don't know." However she learned, I'm grateful that she did. I've watched her strength, courage and unerring good judgment shine through her children and I'm proud of her beyond words.

In my case, like building a strong fort, I laid brick upon brick of assurance about my ability *to know*, until one day a flaw at the bottom of that wall gave way and the whole facade fell. Our younger daughter fell seriously ill with depression. Suddenly, I ran out of answers and surrendered to that fact.

I'm happily content now to seek information, ask questions, use my intuition and imagination, but without the urgency of immediate response to others or myself. I don't whisper. I say out loud, with strength, pleasure and freedom, "I don't know."

To Act or Not, That Is the Question

To move on or not, that is the question. I am sitting in the middle of a sandstorm, a regular occurrence in West Texas, my eyes closed, hands over my face. I can't determine how widespread the storm is, don't know its perimeters. It could be just a small whirlwind. I can choose to sit it out, just remain where I am, with the stinging sand surrounding me. Or, I can choose to get up and start walking. Sooner or later, I will emerge from the storm.

Having life blowing around me, flinging sand in my face, is scary. The natural inclination is to just sit down and endure, hands covering my face. At times this seems the only choice.

Perhaps I do need to sit awhile, get my bearings, think out my plan. Eventually, action might be the best solution to the storms of life. It takes a courage I may not feel to let go of my present moorings. Letting go of what I think is my security, moving into the unknown is intimidating. I didn't expect this interruption; I had no idea it was going to descend. Now my careful preparations are thrown into limbo.

I can rage over my powerlessness, protest, proclaiming, "This isn't fair!" But eventually, self-preservation calls me to acceptance. What is, is. No more, no less. Now what can I do, what is a possible action to take? Is there one?

There may be a time in life for the decision to change my direction. I will feel it intuitively. It isn't necessary to know where this move will take me. It isn't necessary to deduce the outcome. Most of the time I will not know. This is where trust is exercised—trusting that inner urge. If the move turns out to be less than helpful, I can usually go back to where I was, with little lost. But if the move results in breaking out of the storm, how empowering this will feel. I had the courage; I had the follow-through.

There are times to sit in quiet acceptance and times to move out. Today I use my discretion and intuition to judge which road is the more appropriate.

Life is full of storms. But there is a lesson in each. Something we are called upon to recognize and deal with, to learn from. Something calls me into change, into growth, calls me to stretch myself, ascending into another level of consciousness, to accept the challenge.

Scars and Bruises

The angry red scar on my left knee will not go away. It should have healed by now since it's been a year, but there it is, still an indignant red. So maybe there's an assignment. At the very least it serves as a reminder. The reminder is that many times I carry around scars that won't heal because I can't forgive and forget the cause of the injury or the person who inflicted it.

At my age I boast quite a few scars. Some are not visible like the one on my knee. These invisible scars are those of the constant drip of loss—losses ranging from youth, jobs, homes, loved ones and companions, and finally the time when I'll lose some functioning of my body.

Some internal bruises result from growing-up traumas, some from the relationship battlefield. The most frightening of these word-wounds come from those spoken "for your own good," some in the name of God. I'm thinking of the subtle insinuations that I could be more than I am, that if only I would worship God as the people speaking to me worship God, then I'd be okay. When the Bible is used as a weapon, the judgment from others inflicts wounds.

Topical treatments as well as antibiotics abound for external cuts. But for the inner scars and bruises, I can think of only one remedy: forgiveness. Like a warm liquid, forgiveness melts hurt like butter on hot pancakes.

There really are no other remedies for these inner hurts. At first it appears easier to hold the pain inside waiting for the opportunity to get even. But the energy required to haul around old anger pushes me along like an icy glacier, scraping and scarring grooves of unforgiveness, etching them on my soul.

I would rather be at peace than be right. I'd rather be released from the automatic victimization that comes with blame. I can choose to move on. I can choose to forgive.

Major/Minor

I play the piano. My favorite tunes have always been those with predominately minor chords. It is in the contrast with major chords that they ring out with special beauty.

Life too, seems to present us with both—the major and the minor. In retrospect, it seems to me that the minor has contributed tremendously to my growth. I've learned so much in life from "minor" people—people who appear for a short time to deliver the message, whatever it is, then drift away.

It seems to me that the simple, humble people in life often win the inner contest, walking with serenity in this frantic world. When I was attending a meeting held in a downtown church basement, a quiet, gentle appearing man walked in and sat down. He had not attended the meeting previously. His clothes indicated that he might possibly belong to the group of homeless people who frequented the churchyard. The subject of the meeting turned to belief, trust in God. Most of the group said they were seeking a deeper connection with God and many people raised their hands and spoke. This perhaps homeless man who had walked in raised his hand. In a quiet voice he said, "Seems to me, there's only two things you need to know about God. One, there is a God, and two, it ain't you." Such simplicity, spoken with utter humility. We never saw him again. But his simple statement has stayed with me through the years. I think about that humble soul often.

In Scripture, Jesus did not hang out with the people who were wealthy and powerful, the major chords in life. It was with the minor, insignificant, weak, the sinners, that he found ears capable of hearing his message. It was not with the ones who were considered most holy, most educated, most religious that Jesus could speak his truth. Perfect trust was found with the minors of the world. They were the ones who embraced the new belief system of love with courage. The willingness to listen and change came with those who had little or nothing to lose.

It is from the occasional cab driver, the waitress at the corner café, the boy who sacks my groceries, that I receive the biggest smiles and the courtesy so lacking in everyday life. One day after a visit from a furniture repairman, I shut the door and smiled. We had talked about his work into which he poured his artistic self. Matching and mixing his colors with the different shades of furniture, he expertly painted over scratches and dents. Without charge, he then fixed other items in my home that he saw needed repair. He painted, I watched, and we talked about values and beliefs. After his departure, I was left with a sense of the generous gift he had given of himself.

Also, seemingly minor, insignificant decisions have turned out to be decisive. A spur-of-the-moment decision to attend one session of summer school in Colorado rippled its effects later in my life, because the boy I met during that semester reappeared in my life thirty years later. This minor decision to attend summer school in Colorado turned out to be a major blessing in my life. This man with whom I connected during that summer long ago became my second husband.

As the years go by, I find beauty in the minor everywhere. Less *is* more. The less I have, the less I have to take care of and worry about. It is with the smallest amount packed that traveling is made easier. Keeping my schedule simple helps with fading energy levels.

I will always look for treasures in the minor chords of life.

The Value of Silence

If I am talking and there is no one to hear the words, do I exist? If I am silent, do I exist? The art of talking and listening is the way we communicate and feel alive. How often that process goes awry.

Many forms of communication run off track. I've long wondered how some people cannot seem to stop talking. It's not that these people are uncaring. They can be loyal, loving friends, full of good intentions; but I part from their company feeling stuffed with conversation to which I didn't contribute much, if anything. I know I've been guilty of over-talking myself. Especially when I feel out of touch with myself, uncomfortable in my own skin, I tend to talk too much.

Equally as prevalent is the habit of instant reference back to ourselves. Recently, while telling a friend of an event that happened to me, instead of actively listening, she immediately referred to a similar experience in her life. Like a broken string of pearls, the connection was ruptured, and I couldn't figure out how to restring the pearls of communication.

However, as I've grown older, the value I place on silence has increased. There is peace in silence—a quiet pause to reflect. There is so much outer distraction, so much bombardment of the senses today, too much information. Silence has taken a back seat.

Growing up in the work-ethic era, I had to be sick in bed or traveling on an airplane to read in the daytime without guilt. Spending time silently, still, seemed a selfish waste of time. The freedom of silence is often looked upon with distaste and fright. We feel we have to be accomplishing something—unthinkable to not utter a word during our day. Certainly life rightly demands conversation; but the opportunity for quiet can somehow be carved out of our day, even if it's only for a short period. It benefits others as much as ourselves, because we return to our families, our communities, our friends with renewed energy and balance.

The benefits of silence, of sitting, of empting the mind doesn't have an instant payoff. I suppose that might explain the scarcity of participation. I have made this time available, to not indulge the inner voice commanding, "Get busy." This silent time has delivered immense rewards. A gentle ease, a grounding of my inner self, and a congruence of my thoughts, feelings, and actions follow. They flow unimpeded. And I find it easier to say what I mean and mean what I say with equanimity.

The world does not care about silence and only grudgingly grants this permission. I value me enough to give it to myself. I *do* exist and exist more peacefully, when I find time for silence.

Illuminating the Way

I like to think of my body as a candle, the wick—my soul. This candle is the only one I will have throughout my life. Sometimes my wick flickers when life overwhelms me. Problems surface and persist. Mishaps pile on top of each other. My light wavers.

Candles can be tall, strong ones or small and fragile. Candles come in all colors and shapes but the size, shape, or color of the candle doesn't matter because it is the wick that radiates light.

We all know the phrase, "Let your light shine forth," but at times that's a tall order. Occasionally, I'm not even sure my "light" is there. Situations crowd out the belief that I have something worthwhile to shine forth during dark times.

I have a feeling that most of us don't know to what extent our light shines forth. Certain days show up when it seems there's no light to show for myself, let alone for others. But occasionally a person approaches and comments on something I've said that helped them. What a blessing to understand that even unaware and without motive, I've touched a life in a positive way.

Sometimes I see, especially during the Christmas season, plastic candles, with electric bulbs mimicking candlelight. Although they will burn long into the night, indeed, burn until the bulbs go out, they provide no warmth. In real life, the candlelight is not steady and uninterrupted as it is in artificial bulbs. In real life, the wick can burn low while at other times its light is steady and strong. These variances occur because the wick is authentic.

There is a reason for my existence and yours. Each of us is a teacher. I've learned some of the most important lessons in life from the most surprising sources. I've learned about excitement and awe, trust and truth through the eyes of my grandchildren. I've learned patience and compassion from those difficult to be around. I believe we humans reflect light here and there, and just as I learn from all, so also might I illuminate a path for others.

Out of Darkness Comes Light

I was afraid in the dark. As a child, a night-light in my room was a necessity. And even now, having finished my child-rearing years and living alone, I leave a kitchen cabinet light on at night. It offers a small contribution of light to the darkness of an entire apartment.

Underlying the fear of darkness is fear of the unknown. Now I see; now I don't. The illusion of thinking I know what exists "out there" is persistent. I go about my daylight hours totally unaware of questions that surface with the darkness. Fears looms after the sun goes down.

Someone wise once told me to make friends with my fears, to welcome the questions, the doubts, as guests in my home, in my mind. Indeed it seems that my most important lessons have not come from the light, the successes in life, not from the gifts bestowed from the even hand of benign fate, but from the darkness of the soul.

It is from the acceptance of not knowing that I enjoy peace. Freedom comes from not having to have answers, explanations, not insisting on logical reason. The letting go of fear, resting in the questions, living without answers, are powerful gifts. The groundwork for this miracle was a conscious choice: a choice to believe in God's goodness, in his presence, and in the basic goodness of the universe, regardless of its appearance.

It's not as if I awoke one morning saying to myself, "I'm going out today and accept God's plan for my life." It didn't come that way. This benevolent gift from On High was handed me by grace. It was nothing I did, nothing I worked for. It materialized out of the total darkness of grief, of sadness and mourning, the loss of everything I thought I had to have to live. It arrived from willingness to believe.

Earthquake after earthquake shook my life, removing from existence those people who made up my security—my family. One after another disappeared through death: my mother, my second husband after only six years, a son, and a daughter. There was no base line to return to, no sense of my universe anymore. I was in total darkness.

I let go then, yielded. Nothing more was possible for me to figure out, no more pieces to place neatly into my life-puzzle. By releasing preconceived beliefs of how things should be, I was free to form a new pattern, a new world. I quit fighting—anything and anyone. Whatever is, let it come, I said deep inside. And, of course, it did come and I was graced by a willingness to trust again and I saw my world with different eyes. Not a world of pain and woe, but a world of grace and lessons learned.

Occasionally I depend emotionally upon my surviving son and daughter and their families. What precious gifts they are. I thank God every day for each of them. And when fear rears its ugly head about their safety, I remind myself that we are all right at this minute, and today is all any of us have. My job is to remain receptive for this one day. My instructors will appear if I'm open. And difficult as it is, I have to let go of the illusion of control. I can't lock any person into place, can't nail my security to the floor.

I write down on paper what I've learned from the lightness and what I've learned from darkness, and so often it is the darkness that holds the treasure.

Hidden Treasures

All kinds of treasures are hidden in the black box that sits on my desk—my computer. There it sits quietly holding unbelievable jewels about literally everything, a wealth of surprises and information But I must have a key to access this bounty. I have to discover how to open the doors of information and be willing to learn new skills.

To open my mind to what is "new" takes willingness, flexibility, and belief—mainly belief that it's possible for me to learn new skills, belief that it's possible for me to put aside my old typewriter to make room for new technology. I discover that access to computer treasures is not only through purchasing a computer, but also through books and teachers, classes and practice.

I'm like my computer—treasures lie buried inside of me too. Just as with my computer, some of these gifts lay untapped, unseen until recognized and called upon. My willingness to explore is the key to opening these treasures inside me—the willingness to seek the intangible, the unseen, without prejudice, and to believe there is something of unique value deep inside. The path to these stored jewels is through need, usually desperate, and the personal experience that follows. It involves turning loose, trusting that there resides within all of us a permanent place for a benevolent God and his silent gifts.

Access to God's hidden power seems to be delivered through humility, need, longing, and through the realization that I alone am not enough for the task of living. Only then can I ask for the consciousness to feel the presence and help of the Unseen.

When I released self-sufficiency, I found what it took to uncover the inner treasures that I myself did nothing to put there. And these are the treasures that God can use. With them I can be of service.

Like the computer, the riches that reside within us are available to all who seek. It is a choice. I choose to seek. I'm looking to believe. It is saying to God, "I'm here, my eyes are open, please show me the way, show me my gifts, and tell me what to do with them."

What Is, Is

At times I feel as if I have fallen into the bottom of the well. Those are the days that come to all of us, when the veil of security and well-being, the sense that everything is fine flies out the window. Problems erupt and swell to unbearable proportion and every situation looms gigantic, unmanageable. On less severe days, it just seems the sun is dulled and I am submerged in self. On these days I've learned to ask myself the question, "What illusion are you living in today?"

It seems to me that life is comprised of the inner image we harbor, which may be an illusion. One illusion that seems most common for me is, "I shouldn't have losses, shouldn't have disappointments, and shouldn't have pain." "Why me," I ask. When the more realistic question is, "Why not me?"

Who constructed the veil of denial and falsehood that life should be proceeding well because I'm trying? The answer is that *I* did. I constructed it. I bought into the belief early on that life was always going to be beautiful, the 1950's vision of the all-American family, the happy wife and mother. It should *look* like this, and furthermore, it should *stay* like this. And I played the pretend game.

I did this until one day the veil of illusion fell, the deteriorating hooks upon which it had hung all those years finally broke and I was left with reality. What a shock. While I was wearing the veil, I'd wondered out loud, "Goodness, look at the people around me who have all these problems." Suddenly "all these people" turned out to be me.

That was my entry into what is, is. No more "shoulds" and "oughts" to isolate and protect me. No more pretense. It took work on my inner self to come to the solid acceptance that each day presents opportunities to learn and that problems exist as teachers. Did I like this? No. But I did learn that the harder I fought reality, the more uncomfortable I became.

Okay. So, let go.

Easy to say. Hard to do. The self that wants what it wants and wants it now still surfaces. If I can remain in the process of looking at reality and surrender to what is, how much sharper the vision is. Yes, this vision has rough edges and hard surfaces. But its once blurry picture is now crystal clear! I am now better able to move on. I can sit beside the well rather than plunging in.

Life—Static or Fluid

I love rivers. The endless flow assures that the water will remain fresh. But should the water of the river enter a cove in which there is no exit, the water grows stagnant.

There was a time in my life when I believed that still water was preferable. You get where you want to go and then that's it, you stay there. How human to want to preserve the present comfort forever.

Although there are many people consciously not letting their lives stagnate, the tendency to lock down the comfort of where we are is pervasive in human nature. We achieve a certain level of ease in our jobs, our marriages, our communities, and in our churches and naturally we want to stop right there—hold it just like it is—make the seemingly good situation into an absolute. There it remains until someone recognizes that the once-fresh water has gone stale.

If I hear only what I already know the knowledge becomes static and prevents further learning or growing. If I listen only to that with which I agree, I forfeit the benefit of challenge, of change, of growth.

In high school it used to amaze me to watch a close friend stand up in front of an auditorium and debate. Inside I cringed. I had been raised to "go with the flow," not make waves. It seemed that I would always be this way. But I was fascinated by my friend's courage. I envied her.

It wasn't until I reached middle age that I broke out of the freeze box. It was a process of seeking and learning, and eventually, one morning I awoke to possibilities that had remained hidden for years. I recognized that the barrier to my growth was self-imposed. Timidly at first, I opened new doors and found a fluid, wide world to explore.

I admire sculpture and those that hold the most appeal display action, movement. One that immediately comes to mind is the symbol that my brother, being a Marine, dearly loves—the Marines of World War II hoisting the American flag on foreign soil. Another sculpture that brings a light, buoyant feeling to me is one my friend, Judy, has sitting on the coffee table of her living room—this one in porcelain—depicting two young women in a dance movement. Head back, hair flowing and skirts billowing, the women are connected by joined hands, moving in free and joyous union.

Occasionally, I find people for whom freedom of movement is no longer possible who enjoy this fantastic feeling, for it is a state of mind and spirit that refuses immobility, that rejoices in pushing out and forward, breaking old barriers.

As life moved me forward, I discovered there was more to learn—teachings from life, from nature and the pitfalls that caused me to stumble. In the following chapters, I share more specifically those lessons.

2

Parenting—Letting Go of Perfection

Give Up to Win

Some battles exist that you have to give up to win. But tell that to a Marine! "No way," many might say, "No way am I going to just give up." My father taught me, "Never give up!"

There is a Chinese toy, a colorful braided straw tube into which you put an index finger at each end. Then comes the surprise. When you try to extract your fingers and pull to do so, the tube tightens its hold. The more you pull, the tighter it binds. Many of us find it difficult to quit pulling—surely if we just try harder...

In like fashion, when I grapple with a situation or a person, what increases the distress are my thoughts locking in their effort to change things, to make them fit with my own picture of what the situation should look like. As with the Chinese toy, the more I struggle, the tighter I hold the thoughts, the greater my discomfort. I want a different conclusion; see the harvest of my desire. As long as I stay in my intellect, the constriction increases.

At times I have to be forced to release my judgments and predictions, forced to release my tenacious hold, forced to relinquish my attachment—like giving up trying to force a cap on the wrong-sized bottle. For too long I held onto an expectation that medical professionals would help two of my children recover completely from their grave mental illnesses. I was adamant that this would be the result of the doctors' efforts along with mine. But this outcome was not to be—given the state of mental health diagnostic and medication tools at that time. How much has been accomplished in that field since then. My children's lives ended amidst my anguish and protestations. Due to the torment of living with their flawed brain chemistry, they took their lives, something I must carry forever.

The prayer that has offered me relief and abundant peace is the Serenity Prayer by Reinhold Niebuhr:

> God grant me the serenity to
> Accept the things I cannot change,
> The courage to change
> The things I can,
> And the wisdom to know the difference.

What I can change is my acceptance of the many things I cannot change.

Seeds of Growth

I planted flower seeds a few weeks ago. Because I live in a high-rise, my flowers grow in pots on my deck. Each day I look to see if a sprout has appeared. No sprouts yet. Why not, I wonder. My immediate inclination is to dig around in the soil to see if any seeds are sprouting under the surface. I want to will the sprouts to bloom.

I've become aware that this is what I do with important others in my life, especially my children. Like the flower seeds, I want to see in their lives the sprout of growth from the seed of experience I hope I've planted. I sincerely want to protect them as well as other loved ones from wrong roads I've taken, from missteps so clear to me now. I desperately want to share my knowledge and experience.

But I can't. And this is the pain that life presents. It seems a familial fact that I'm most likely the last person to be able to share insights with my family. It appears that the ones I love the most, my children especially, are the last to truly know who I am. Others may ask me for direction, others may appreciate my growth, and follow my path of awareness. But not the ones I care most passionately about.

By this time in life, I'm better about the expectation that they'll profit from my mistakes. While I hope I've let go of this natural inclination, truthfully I know I haven't.

Kahlil Gibran so wisely says in *The Prophet:*

> Your children are not your children.
> You may give them your
> Love but not your thoughts,
> For they have their own thoughts.
> You may house their bodies but not their souls.
> For their souls dwell in the house of tomorrow, which you
> Cannot visit, not even in your dreams.
> You are the bows from which your children as living arrows
> Are sent forth.
> Let your bending in the archer's hand be for gladness;
> For even as He loves the arrow that flies,

So He loves also the bow that is stable.[1]

How arrogant, really, to presume to know the path my young will take, to presume that I have the slightest idea of the road God will place before them. At last it is with freedom from total responsibility that I can rest assured that it isn't all up to me.

The most I can do is be there when asked to be. Stand firmly by the side of these important others with love, with compassion, and an extended hand. I pray to have still lips but a willing, loving heart. I have to wait, just as I wait to see if my seeds will sprout and become flowers.

---

1.   Kahlil Gibran, *The Prophet* (New York, Alfred A. Knopf, Inc, 1923), p. 17.

Beehive for Rent

At times my mind is a beehive, full of frantic activity followed by periods of quiet. Ideas fly in and out accompanied by directions, "Do this, Do that, Make sure that you…" and on and on.

This frenzied urgency stems from an ancient coping strategy—the idea that I am in charge of running the universe. By buying into this idea, I fool myself into believing I will be safe. Each idea and course of action presents three choices: (1) Should have done it yesterday, (2) Do it now, and (3) Wait. It is number three that's the most troublesome. Waiting equals wasting. The impulse to jump right in, expend energy, right now, consumes.

Energy is like money in the bank. There is a finite amount that if rationed appropriately, covers the expenses. The pressure to do things faultlessly and do them now takes a toll on my energy. As I age, my supply of energy wanes. I must withdraw only the necessary energy for that day. What is most important takes precedent; yet how easy it is to extend past my assets and experience.

Complications surface when the beehive takes itself seriously, places itself in the center of the world. Be all to all. I bolt right into the middle of over-responsibility, then suffer the ensuing exhaustion. Trying to fix the universe is like a rock thinking it can push the earth closer to the moon. The belief that I know exactly what should be done for anyone, especially family and friends, gives off the unmistakable scent of arrogance that drives loved ones away.

Complicated thinking and over-planning finally cave in to reality. What exactly can I control? Very little. Usually I find peace in pausing, then only doing the right thing that appears before me in the next moment. Spiritual reading tells me to lead an honorable life and take care of myself so that I will be able to care for others when it's time. More important, I must wait to share my experience until asked.

There's that "wait" again! Why do I feel that if I don't make it happen, it won't? Where is my faith that others have their own paths, that there is purpose in every event? The thinking that if I don't force the situation it won't happen confronts me with my longing to control. As usual, the real requirement is to let go. Let go of expectations, let go of planning the outcome, let go of making things happen. With this practice the thought, "If only," fades.

With a tranquil mind, a still beehive, comes the larger response that soothes and comforts: "Enough for now. Be still and wait." The emergency of the moment relaxes and that little voice inside sighs and says, "Oh, good!"

Head Up, Young Person

A scene in a movie I watched portrayed a mature woman teaching a dance class. A young male student kept looking down at his feet while practicing the steps. The teacher's reminder to him was simple, "Head up, young person." So prompted, he immediately raised his head.

I go back in time and remember my children's struggles to learn the dance steps to life, to grow into maturity. My wish was a path of ease for each, an uncomplicated route through the maze of growing up.

More than one of my children chose paths fraught with problems and dangers, some of these problems were the result of capricious genetics. The parent in me wanted to set the best course for each child—wishful thinking. The truth was I could only guide, suggest, and pray. I agonized over choices they made. I lamented their consequences, and a part of me held myself responsible. Wasn't I supposed to stand in protection from every pitfall?

Again, the knowledge hit me on the head—I could not play God. These precious children came through me but they were not mine. There was a path they were destined to take in order to learn specific lessons that had nothing to do with me. Though a tough task, I removed my responsibility hat.

The best I could do after these children became adults was to offer my support, and always, my love. Like God's love for us, there is nothing they can do to make me love them less, and nothing they can do to make me love them more than I already do. I can cheer them on when they are filled with doubt and despair. I can say, "Head up, young person. This too shall pass."

The Hand We're Dealt

All of us are dealt a hand in life. The one I get is the one I have to play. I can't exchange it, ask God for a different hand. Like some card games, the hand of life is dealt face down. Most of us will stare at the facedown cards and imagine we know just what they will reveal when turned over.

There is a career card, a card for love, a card for marriage, and a card for each child. The illusion is that we think we know for sure what each card will reveal. For instance, the career one will be a high spade. The love card will be a heart, right? But experience reveals that some of those love cards will not be hearts, in some hands they may be clubs. Suppose we have a daughter or son card and we know that it will be a Queen or King of Hearts, Diamonds at least. We have no doubt about this. That is what they are.

With much excitement we will turn our life cards over at the appropriate time. To our delight, some of the cards will be higher than anticipated. We might find an ace instead of the expected ten. What perhaps we didn't realize was that these cards become our lessons in life, as specific and individual as fingerprints.

I'm in trouble if I insist upon one card, one area of my life, being just as I imagine it. Try as I might, I cannot convert a club into a diamond. And the harder I fight for what I want, the more it evades me—like trying to force a river in another direction, or straining to make someone the replica of my fantasy. The key to a winning hand is acceptance.

A "good" life hand isn't the one with the highest numeric score. The winning hand is any hand received as is and played to the best of one's ability. My life's cards eventually become a game with myself—not a competition with others. I must discard the illusion that my hand is better or worse than another's if I'm to have peace. It's my game. No one can play my hand for me. The way I play my hand brings joy and comfort or sadness and regret.

Eventually I come to the understanding that I wouldn't trade hands with anyone. My cards, my lessons are specific to my needs. They are the catalyst to correct my faulty thinking, teach me how to attain the peace and the joy I desire.

My wish is to allow myself to recognize the truth that lies in my hand, accept it, and work with it. I can't change the cards but they will fit into the game of life with ease as long as I have acceptance.

Requirement: Do Nothing With Love

Parenting! A measureless gift, yet at times a heavy weight. My mother taught me that being a caretaker was the highest goal for a woman. Even in early childhood, I lived with the expectation that I was to take care of her, her feelings and her problems. I was her confidant, indeed her "life" she told me. I became aware of her every mood and I saw myself in charge of them. Happy, sad, angry—I had a part. This pseudo control at first made me feel powerful, but eventually turned toxic.

I learned to be vigilant concerning others, watchful of their moods, and adjusted myself to ease whatever situation I found myself in. I continued employing this radar system without thought of its consequences.

Although much later I came to see how exhausting and debilitating this was, even today I can slip into the old habit of trying to ease situations for others which display tension. It's as natural as breathing. The thing is, I truly do care about others. I genuinely care about their well-being and their happiness. I especially want the best for my loved ones.

The dilemma is to weed out caring from controlling. The key for me was discovering the arrogance hidden in this way of life. It's quite simple. I'm not God. If I believe, as I say I do, that God does not have any grandchildren, we are all his children, if I can truly entrust myself into his care, why can I not trust that he is in the lives of my loved ones also? Finally it comes down to the reality that I by myself am not in charge of anything or anybody but myself. The things I try to control in the name of "caring" will turn out as they're going to turn out anyway. As a wise friend of mine says to herself, "Wait. You don't have a dog in that fight." The reality is that control is out of my control.

Parents are supposed to guide and protect their young. But I was not prepared for the most important part of parenting—the letting go, the releasing of my babies to fly out of the nest and forge their own way. My urge to protect and promote good persisted well past the stage of life when I should have been released from this duty. I clung to my patterns, finding the same admonitions and cautions flowing through my veins and out of my mouth. Before I could engage my mind, the stagnant flow of old words would pour out.

But eventually, clarity came. Taking the heavy mantle of responsibility off my shoulders released energy for being fully present for others. I'm not responsible for the circumstances in which loved ones find themselves. A card bearing this message is fixed on my refrigerator, so I am reminded daily: "Do Not Feel Totally, Personally, Irrevocably Responsible for Everything. That is My Job. Love, God."

It seems that doing nothing with love is actually doing quite a lot and leads to peace within. I've developed a mantra for myself when I visit my grown children and their families. It's simple. I say to myself: "Nothing is required of you at this time." What a comforting fact. All I do is present myself with love and try to remain quiet. As someone once said, "A closed mouth gathers no feet."

Help Is Out There

A young mother walked towards me in the park with great strides, almost running, her arms swinging. From a distance I could see a navy blue bunching of cloth in the middle of her chest. As I came closer it was apparent that the bundle was a tiny baby, wearing a pink sun hat on its little head. It was facing the mother, arms and legs dangling.

This mother looked very young—I thought perhaps this was her first baby. As I watched her approach, it worried me that the baby was strapped so close to her mother's chest, face forward, her head encased in the sunbonnet. Could she breathe? Remembering back to my own child rearing, our babies were seldom taken on walks or runs. And I remembered my feelings of overwhelm with my first child. I too was very young and I didn't know anything about rearing a child. Society does little to foster mandatory parenting education. We become parents, usually at an early age, expecting ourselves to be proficient at these skills. And we usually simply follow the road map our parents gave us by example. Thus we fall into a do-to-ours-as-was-done-to-us trap, or the opposite of the same coin: Do it all differently.

I thought about what this scene also depicted to me—the parent/ child bond that can flourish to be one of love and closeness without infringement on the child's being. Or it could tighten, eventually enveloping and restraining the child. Holding on, letting go, the lessons life teaches.

We are also called upon to allow our children to fall occasionally, to fail. For a parent this is difficult to watch. We want to do our job—assuring perfect safety for our children. We demand this impossible goal from ourselves. But certainly I learned from stumbling and having to right myself again. Parenting is probably the most important job any of us will have. I've been astounded looking back about how little I knew going into this adventure. Seeking advice, getting counseling about navigating these new channels wasn't on my radar screen in the 50's or 60's. And I fell into other ways of coping with my deeply felt inadequacy.

The mark of intelligence to me is the willingness to acknowledge a lack of experience and seek the advice of those with necessary information. Many parents cannot bring themselves to the humble admission that alone they do not have the expertise, to ask for help. There is information out there. There are people who have far more data and experience to which we may turn. Would that we have the courage to seek it, for our children's sake.

3

Addiction—Road Block

From Judy, With Love

As a little girl, the person I loved to imitate above all others was Judy Garland. I bought all her records, saw her every show, even bought a 5x7 glossy picture of her as Dorothy skipping down the yellow brick road. Little did I know that I might share more with Judy than the love of singing.

As I grew up, so did Judy. She developed a strong, vibrating voice that said it all for me. I felt life in her voice, felt courage in the songs she belted out. I would sing along to her recordings, arms open, face lifted, mimicking her delivery.

"Somewhere Over The Rainbow," recalled the soft and dreamy me. "Clang, Clang, Clang Went the Trolley," represented the excited me.

And, "The One Who Got Away," I secretly sang to the boy in math class who noticed me but dated someone else.

So I danced and sang with Judy, strolling around my bedroom with an imaginary microphone in my hand, until my mother would call upstairs asking me to please turn the music down. Even after I turned from this enticing make-believe world to the homework world, inside I remained Judy for at least another hour.

There was an energy and a passion about Judy, an expectation, a throw-your-whole-being-into-a-song about her, a big YES to life about her. She was my role model for living with gusto and feeling, a proud, courageous walk in the world. She was a heroine to me.

But somewhere along the way, Judy fell into the pit of addiction—an illness that eventually took her life. What a loss, for her, for us. Watching her life presented on television, I saw the perfect depiction of the pain and loneliness suffered by an addict. I could feel the tightening of the ropes that bound her, squeezing out her life force. She went from being a bright, shiny singer bouncing with life, energizing those around her, to a miserable, nervous, self-centered diva.

No finger of blame need be pointed, because it doesn't matter how or who, where or why. Solid lessons remain for all of us. Lessons of what happens to gifts of spirit when the wires get crossed, forcing one into coping mechanisms that prove disastrous. Lessons in taking control of our lives, not permitting others to exploit, use or abuse us. Lessons in how unrelenting and persistent addiction is, lessons about the masks used to hide the problem, in the separation from God, from people, and from ourselves that follow the road to addiction. This road has no pretty yellow bricks.

I am reminded of the value and strength of total surrender. Judy could not or would not recognize the dead end; she could not or would not allow the powerful persona she had created to disappear in the saving waters of submission. I was more fortunate. The snare of addiction caught me as well. But Judy's path signaled to me and helped me make different choices early in my life. Her death from addiction remains a strong and insightful revelation, a stark picture of lost hope. And that was her gift to me. Perhaps it will be to others as well.

Perfect Gift

Searching for just the right gift. What to purchase for someone who has everything, and yet internally, nothing. This person whom I love with all my heart has had a problem for some time. A problem that doesn't go away by itself. Nor does it go away with the efforts of others. Even the attempts of doctors and ministers seldom produce sustained results. The problem is addiction.

This malady starts out looking benign, a friendly monkey to play with and enjoy, and one who accompanies you everywhere. He's always with you, never leaving your side. Time passes and the monkey that began as company now becomes demanding. Your once cute little companion presses and presses until you dread having him around but can't bring yourself to let him go.

So, strange as this dance becomes, on it goes. The music turns from light and airy to sour and heavy. One goes to bed hoping the dance has ended for our loved one, only to wake to the leftover strains of its tune.

We who watch this foreign dance, even those of us who have shared this peril but have been blessed with recovery, stand paralyzed, puzzled, and afraid. When we voice logical arguments, our frustration turns to grief because our loved one reacts with anger and indignation. Soon regular periods of not speaking increase, and when we do speak, misunderstandings usually result. Now days and nights are fraught with advancing tension.

This dance might continue until the one trapped by the monkey of addiction tires and becomes sick—very sick. The struggle ends temporarily when hospital stays show up in the picture. In the not-yet-ready addict's mind, he is always in the hospital for a reason other than substance abuse. But hope dissolves into disappointment when the monkey we all thought medically removed returns with a clawing vengeance.

Then, for a fortunate few, from out of nowhere, reality breaks through and reaches the fatigued and ill mind. It's as if a tidal wave displaces the old world as our loved one awakens to a new world. Gone is the monkey, the confusion and the civil war inside. A new, calm, assured person immerges. God has apparently answered our years of prayer for this person.

Like a blind patient awakening from surgery with sight, a new reality appears—a new reality for all of us. The person who was lost is now found. It appears that God himself has adjusted the lenses in the glasses through which our loved one views the world. The smile becomes real; the old humor returns.

So, what Christmas gift do I buy for my special loved one this year? In an office supply store my eyes light upon the perfect item. I take it home and gift-wrap it. I take it to my very important person.

When he opens it, a wide smile breaks over his face. He laughs and hugs me. "Perfect," he says, as he places the small paper shredder on his desk. "I know just what to do with this…shred my past."

Have You Seen Me?

Once a week the mail brings a bulletin with pictures and the caption: "Have You Seen Me?" Usually the pictures are of children, sometimes-young adults. All have disappeared from their former lives.

Addiction, like a kidnapper, robs us of our loved ones. Familiar features, posture, and behavior of loved ones with addiction, illness, or trauma at times makes us peer at the family member or friend and wonder the same thing, "Where did you go?" The longer the condition remains untreated, the less definition there seems to be in the facial features. If one looks through old photos, the affected face and body look progressively blurred; somehow the edges are no longer sharp. Just as their memory is fading away, their essence is fading away.

I believe we are what we think, and we live what we believe. When the body and/or mind are diseased or addicted, thinking is skewed, belief systems go awry. Actions that follow carve deep grooves in the soul. The effect on the person becomes obvious over time—the soul has lost its way somewhere inside. There is a decrease in the loved one's "presence."

I've seen before and after recovery pictures of the ill and the addicted. Often there is a stunning difference. Before the illness came, the pictures reveal an aliveness, an awareness, especially in the eyes. During the onset of the problem, pictures show the soul's confusion, the inner war raging. Gradually, as addiction or illness pervades and entrenches, a physical fading from the world scene occurs. "Not present" is facially advertised.

Emerging from mental illness or addiction, the after-recovery pictures are astounding. There is a sharpening of the features, an I-am-present look in the eyes. The message is clear, "I once was lost, and now I'm found. I once was blind, and now I see." It is truly "Amazing Grace" to watch the well person's soul unfold in all its original, intended beauty.

Heart Knowledge

In a tape from the series titled, "Great Themes of Paul: Life as Participation," Father Richard Rohr says that rational knowledge has a ceiling to it and to be led through the hole in the ceiling is the work of God. He says, "Great things cannot be explained by the mind—the heart world is much bigger. Spiritual consciousness is much larger than rational consciousness." [1] In other words, the head alone is limited.

Because those recovering from any addiction often see their lives as before and after, I have a "before and after" division in my life. Early in my life I was swept along in the tide of normalcy, doing things other people did, following the thinking of others, assuming their values, morals and beliefs to be my own. And it was enough, I thought, for a full and happy life.

By my late thirties, this way of life stopped working. I was no longer comfortable continuing the life I'd led following the crowd. I found myself building a dependence on alcohol, beginning with the habit of having a drink every night before dinner, just as my parents had always done. My need for this increased without my awareness until its effects undermined my peace of mind. Outwardly, I appeared a fully functioning adult. But inside the landscape changed into one of depression and misery. One or two drinks would unleash tears of despair. I was not able to pinpoint the cause for the crying, but these periods of sadness turned into a nightmare. Unable to completely stop either the drinking or the crying, I finally connected the pain with the alcohol.

The veil of denial fell away it seemed overnight. A moment of clarity sprang forth and I fell through the clouds into reality. I became aware that my methods of coping with life were not only inadequate, but of greater significance, they were destructive. The temporary, friendly comforter—alcohol—morphed into the enemy, erecting a barrier not possible for God to penetrate.

---

1.   Richard Rohr, O.F.M., *Great Themes of Paul, Life as Participation* (Cincinnati, Ohio, Saint Anthony Messenger Press, 2002, series of ten tapes)

When finally I could go no further with the game, when anguish bowed my head and spirit, the last house on the block was to give up, to stop the pretense. I gave up—surrendered. The bleakness of that dark night stands out in my memory. In my back yard looking at the stars, drink in hand, feeling the millstone of life intensely, suddenly I awakened to both the need for surrender and the need for help. There seemed to be a large hole in the center of my being that nothing could fill. Having nowhere else to go, I bowed my head and asked God for help. I claimed my inadequacy to face life and reality. I had no game plan.

Following that moment of surrender came an immediate lightness, a letting go, a quiet knowledge—becoming apparent much later—that God's direction was trustworthy. That night I became willing to be put on a different road. A plan was placed before me to follow, one that I have continued to travel. Finding peace took time, but that was what I had—time.

But mere surrender was not enough. I found I had to talk about it to someone who would understand. God provided the road signs to a community of kindred souls and I began the process of coming to. There I found an informal setting of other imperfect human beings who opened their arms and heart to me. This community was a different setting from the traditional cathedral of worshipers I'd been familiar with. There was none of the judgment or condemnation I'd found in other settings of worship. These people who shared my experience told me they would love me until I could love myself.

What freedom to have someone listen without judgment to how I felt, what I had done or left undone. It was through this program that I woke up, pop! into reality and into full consciousness. The flat brain wave of depression registered its first blip on the screen of my life.

This division in my lifeline stands out in clarity today—the before and after. I look back in wonder at who that clueless young woman was. Clearly not the person I am today. Gone is the effort to pretend adequacy by going along the bottomless ruts traveled by others before me. Gone are most of the deep insecurities, the ingrained doubts of my own worth. In this miraculous clearing of sight, a renewed sense of awe opened within and remains today.

I am home. And home is the place where my eyes rest easy and my mouth turns up in a smile. I find myself smiling in awe at the crab apple trees in full bloom in the spring. I smile at the ducks crossing the lake in the park. And I smile when my eyes rest on the snow-capped mountains of Colorado. It is a feeling of oneness with everyone and everything. God has opened a hole for me in the ceiling, and there I find a new awareness that I am no longer separate and apart. It was not head knowledge that showed me the way home, but rather that of the heart—the before and the after are sharply delineated.

From this point in my journey, the picture of wholeness broadened to include a world full of others. And slowly the process began of finding, not differences, but similarities between this world of people and me. This is the knowledge of the heart.

Birds of a Feather

Birds of a feather do indeed flock together. I've noticed on my walks through the park that geese gather in one corner of the lake while ducks congregate in a different spot. The ducks and the geese sailing around the lake look like battalions of ships sailing off, one after the other; but usually, they'll come to rest in the midst of their kin.

And don't we do that also? Most of us like to hang out with others who share our ideas, our community, people of like mind. It's comfortable, familiar, and little effort need be expended to sustain our place there.

A reassuring, supportive, common environment can be found in the rooms of the twelve-step programs. Though the disease of addiction is shared, they are not cookie-cutter images. Like an artist mixing colors before painting, in those rooms the hues are always changing, presenting different shades and forms of humanity. Some figures are shadowy, some dark, but there are also splashes of red, a flash of yellow, contributing colors so vibrant they belie the existence of illness. What a wonderful kaleidoscope! Here is a lovely Indian woman with a ruby on her forehead, there a the young man in blue jeans, his crossed leg pumping energetically up and down as he waits his turn to speak. There is the gentle older black man in tattered clothes whose lined face somehow emanates an acceptance of life as it is, a lawyer on his lunch break, and the young housewife with large anguished eyes, open to receiving help, guidance and direction.

No matter their color or age, their name, their religion—all share a common bond—addiction. Their paths will bring them—through pain—priceless gifts that will emerge with time, beginning with the recognition that they are not alone. The price of admission depends upon their willingness to surrender, to find something of larger importance than self, a desire for a new and better life, a wider expanse of horizons heretofore so narrow, and the seeking of peace through service and dependence on a Higher Power. What a beautiful game plan for life the common bond of addiction can offer when we are ready to learn.

The need to find a common bond seems basic to human nature. But the bond doesn't depend on outer appearance. It seems the inner life is what attracts. At our core, we seek likeness of inner need, like perhaps the birds of a feather seek.

When I hear of people living a solitary life, a life of a recluse, my mind and heart struggle to understand how that life can be comfortable. It wouldn't be something I could endure because of my hunger for affiliation, my need of connection to others. The next chapter speaks more about this need.

4

I Need You

Importance of Affiliation

Connection to others ebbs and flows. It's like flying an airplane. When the weather is perfect we effortlessly find our path through the skies and land at our appointed place smoothly. Then there are days when the weather is cloudy, worse, days when the weather is tumultuous and scary, lightening and thunder echoing through the sky. Flying then is less than a breeze.

On the days of bad weather, most of the time flights take off anyway. In life, too, we often show up as anticipated. We arise, dress, and go out to meet the day because it is expected, even when we don't feel quite up to the task.

Relationships have their own weather patterns. Some days it's easy to form connections. Verbal communications flows. At other times, it's cloudy, or stormy, and it's as if we get off the air controller's guiding "beam." We're uneasy with others.

I heard once that loneliness is enduring the presence of one who does not understand.

For me, those are the days that call for a reduction in activity. A slowing down, breathing deeply. Knowledge that tomorrow may be better. It will change. This is a time for letting go of expectations of myself and those I'm with when we're not connecting, our conversation a bit rocky with our emotional air currents. To allow myself mistakes, to be gentle with myself and those around me. As I stay quiet and accepting, I find I am drifting back on the beam of connection. The clouds part and I can relax into the flight of friendship.

Common Mercies

So many street people. I walk right by them. Yes, I do. But while my feet keep walking, my heart stays behind with them. I can't imagine not knowing from day to day if I will eat or where I will sleep. I can't imagine not having someone come look for me to bring me home. I hear comments about "those people" as if they were a different species.

One bag lady remained glued to my mind. She pushed a grocery cart loaded with what appeared to be rags and sacks. Her shoulders were hunched under her bent gray head; and when she looked up, I saw china blue eyes, their blueness startling. Arriving home, I couldn't evict her from my mind. I saw her as a child sitting at the kitchen table in some city, eating dinner, her mother saying, "Eat your carrots." Surely someone must have tucked her in bed and said a prayer over her at least once. Taught her to brush her teeth and tie her shoes. Did she go to school like other children? Did she have brothers or sisters? Where was everybody now? What had happened for life to turn so bleak? Did she have any hopes left? Plans of any kind? Somewhere in her past was there a snapshot of her with a family, arms around one another, smiling?

If we are all connected in our humanity, as I believe we are, how was this allowed to happen? Who let her down? How did she disappoint others, fail, and become ostracized from society? So many questions remain unanswered.

Yet I know there is a piece of me in that bag lady with the blue eyes. Just as there is a piece of me in the female executive sitting in an office overlooking the city. Can it be fate that turned one little girl into a bag lady while the other became an executive? Or did they make choices that determined their fate?

I dislike the attitude of those who see "them" over there and "us" over here—separating and classifying individuals into groups of status. If I can find the smallest element of the spirit of God in the small, the poor, the lost, the afflicted, if I can identify and recognize the smallness and poverty in myself, there must be hope that someday mercy can shine through all of us for each other.

Different

There is a wheelchair-bound lady who lives nearby. She has a marvelous attitude of acceptance and is quite independent. In thinking about people who are disabled, I watch how others react. I watch myself react also. Most of us don't know how to help. We don't want to embarrass anyone, don't want to call attention to a disability, so we look the other way, trying to act as if we're involved in thinking about something, or perhaps we try to appear as if we didn't see them. And so, we end up doing that which is most offensive—giving no attention at all.

The world is full of people with handicaps. I've had the opportunity to have them in my own family. I say opportunity because I've found they have much to contribute. My daughter began suffering with mental illness when puberty arrived. These were the days before our medical world began enjoying pharmaceutical intervention. She was eventually handicapped by her illness, unable to live comfortably in the world. I watched people shy away from her, label her. I watched them be critical of that which they didn't understand. Fear seeped into what should have been compassion.

My daughter was my greatest teacher. She taught me about humility, courage and strength as she walked through her difficult days. The hurt from people's ignorance never stopped hurting her, never stopped hurting me. Even some of God's messengers—church pastors and ministers—from whom my daughter sought comfort, eventually turned deaf ears. In the Bible, Jesus talked to the poor, the lepers, the outcasts because He knew they were ready to understand Him. Through their challenges, they were made humble enough to open the doors to their minds and hearts.

I observe how easy it is for us to separate ourselves from the different, the handicapped. We look but do not see the person behind the disability. We don't deliberately mean to wound, but wound we do. It hurts to be singled out. I learned from my daughter how to hold my own head higher as I watched her hold her head high and bear with dignity and composure the subtle rejection. This beautiful young woman would rise every morning to face each troublesome day with heroic courage.

Every time I am tempted to separate myself from others, to imagine myself different, I am called to stop, to open my arms and embrace in my heart those with disabilities with compassion and love. Father Richard Rohr says, "Until we can meet God in the least of his creatures, we do not have the capacity to meet Him at all."[1]

1.   Richard Rohr, O.F.M., *Great Themes of Scripture* (Saint Anthony Messenger Press, 1999, series of eight tapes)

Tether on the Climb

Yesterday I watched a television program on mountain climbing. The climbers were attached to one another by a tether, a protective rope that catches one of the climbers should he slip. Climbs to the top of most difficult heights require teamwork; chances of making it alone are limited. Even professional climbers who have made it to the summit of Mt. Everest make their journey with at least one other person. I can only imagine the comfort of a nighttime conversation on a cold, icy mountain slope when the only thing between the climber and the outdoor rawness is the tent in which they rest and the presence of another.

Just as with climbers, we, too, will go through hardships in our journey through life. Just as there will be storms on a mountain climb, so also will they appear in life. Of that we can be sure. There will be dangers to overcome, fears to be conquered.

I like to think that in each individual climb on the mountain called life, we are indeed tethered to someone for support. Ideally, of all the people we need, family should be the greatest source of strength and assistance to one another. But unfortunately, sometimes this is not the case. Too many times family wounds are slow to heal or do not heal at all. In these instances the tether proves stressed. Fortunately, the possibility of creating strong ties to supportive friends exists in life. Here we can create a tether of safety.

In spite of support, throughout our struggle as we make our way up the mountain of life, there will be wear and tear on the tether, the lifeline that ties us to one another. It might become stretched to the breaking point. It will be tested, rubbed raw against rock time and again. Weathered by the sun, rain, and storms.

No matter the time that goes by, or the stresses of life, I know for a certainty that the tether that binds me to my surviving son and daughter will hold tight, for underneath the frail, weathered rope there remains a strong, golden wire which can withstand anything for it has the strength of abiding love. This strength miraculously holds, for a lifetime.

Friendship Counts

"You will find that one of the most important things in life will be your friends," my Dad told me when I was eight. I learned as much from his example as any spoken word. Gregarious and friendly, my father always had golfing, business, and social friends, and I watched him spending time with them. The joyous aspect to their conversation, the happy, relaxed feeling to their association was inviting. There were no undercurrents, no hidden agendas, no expectations. Just joy in being together, laughing together. These connections were important to my father. He could have any number of people arrive at his side, in full support if need be.

I am like my father in this respect. High on my need list is affiliation, connection. I feel graced with a basic trust of people. While family is extremely important in my life and always has been, I find, like my father, that the misreading of one's intention is more apt to occur in family life. There are issues in family life that lie frozen in the past. The tip of the iceberg hides misunderstandings underneath, sometimes added to through generations unless work is done to undo them. Misinterpretations seem common in family life, and to me, everything is at stake there. I feel I absolutely must have my family's love and devotion.

It seems to me these barriers don't exist as much in healthy friendships. For me, there is less at stake, a freedom of openness, trust that one will be able to communicate with truth, the need for understanding and love naturally assumed.

I follow my father's pattern. I crave the honest, open dialogue that seems easy with friends. As friends do not just drop out of the sky, I work diligently to nurture these connections. I cultivate my garden of friends with interest and sustained effort. I water these gardens regularly, work to eliminate the weeds of neglect and dissention that threaten to choke out the flowers of connection.

My desire to work in the garden of family is no less. I work just as hard in those fields. But in the family rows, I am working with old material. Here and there in these rows there blooms the most beautiful flowers, but here I fear the weather and weeds more. In the fields of family, my work is just as diligent, but the trust that my intentions and love will be noticed and returned is less. And my father's statement that relationships are somehow easier with friends lingers in my mind.

I shall continue my harvesting. I will plow and work both fields, family and friends. In both, the efforts are well worth constant care.

Silence: Weapon or Salve

What you are *not* saying is so loud I cannot hear what you *are* saying.

Silence can be a potent message. It can be comfortable, a rhythmic flow, a restful connection, a silent energy of support, signifying love. It can be an effort to keep another from hurt. Or silence can wound. It can feel controlling, punishing and cold. The absence—the no words, no questions, no comments—at times can be used to admonish or diminish. Silence can represent the deliberate leaving out of another, making a person's presence into a screen, looked through and not seen. There is no pain like being invisible to another. Mostly we judge the warmth or coolness of our partner's silence by our intuition—the lack of verbal communication can feel warm or the silence can feel cold.

Underlying most of our verbal communication or lack thereof is a belief system—an unspoken, subjective focus of the individual. Whenever I'm aware of the wall of no words, I have a choice: I can spend time guessing what the silence means or I can ask for clarification. I can open my mouth and tell the person that I am feeling confused and check it out. I wish that I did this more often. I don't know why this is so hard. Perhaps because I was schooled from my early years to take what I see and hear and ask no questions. I am supposed to know what is going on with the person with whom I'm communicating. But how many times intuition tells me something is very different from how it appears, and silence can intensify this uncertainty.

My need to connect is vital—I desire to be in relation with each person I am with, even though that time might be ever so brief. And the path to that connection is through verbal contact.

I need feedback—someone to feed back to me what they are thinking. I depend upon verbal communication, especially with loved ones. For as George Eliot has said, "What do we live for, if it is not to make life less difficult for each other?" Silence needs clarification just as much as does conversation.

Vive Le Difference

Humanity is a lot like a shopping area. We are different people having different souls, like individual stores lined up on a street. Nothing would be more boring than to have all the stores identical. My eyes glaze over just contemplating this.

As brother and sister, mother and child, your store and mine were built next door to each other. Our souls were constructed that way also, connected to each other by the same warehouse. And although at times it feels that we impinge upon one another, you and I simply feature and package items differently, like gift shops in a mall. There may be ballet slippers and classical music in my collection, and balloons and porcelain clowns in yours. Baseball hats in mine, woolen caps in yours. Neither of us would wish to tear down the wall between us. It is right and proper to maintain our own shops, separately.

In our respective stores I'm sure we both have shelves of friendliness, kindness, and loyalty, shelves with abundant smiles, hugs, and love, behind which lie boxes of compassion, understanding, and tenderness. And surely we both stock a little friendly "small talk," some everyday harmless gossip we'd share with a neighbor. Maybe there's a section with light questions and open interest. I feel sure in our inventories there's a large quantity of humor and laughter. These sought after items provide the oil for daily living and erase the grooves that stress and negative thinking have produced. Usually there is a bench with coils of "slack," cut to order.

Our shops feature intangible items. In mine we find dreams, hopes, and lots of silly playfulness. Your store may feature ambition, competition, and success. Our storefronts have different facades, not better or worse, superior or inferior—just different. Frankly, I am envious of many items you carry in abundance in your store that I don't carry, and perhaps never will. We display individually also. In the front of my store I keep a large container of free-of-charge manners—please's and thank you's. I feature these because they're important to me. They cost nothing but mean so much. Your store features among other things family devotion by the buckets.

I revel in your uniqueness. I appreciate your separateness. And I am fortunate to be constructed next to you, not overlapping, not under-neath, but on the same level, with the uniqueness of you. Like stores in a mall, with different architecture and dressings, we share the com-monality of humanity.

Such is the nature of stores, such is the nature of mankind. Such is the nature of family and friendship. Vive le difference!

Can You Read Me?

My friend, the driver, stopped the car at a red light. Standing on the corner was a man with a pleading look, his mouth turned upward with a half smile. I looked at the sign he held but could not read it because it was upside down. Before I could register this fully and roll down my window to tell him, the light turned green and my friend drove on.

I thought of the pathos surrounding this situation. Isn't this what I do every day? I assume that my signs are readable. I walk around with an expectation that others can read me, read what I need, what my wants and desires are. It would be better if each day we could simply put on a tee shirt, perfect signals going out to others. "Out of sorts." "Angry at the world." "Need affirmations."

Usually if I'm aware, I can pick up vibes about the emotional climate of a friend by her body language. She walks hesitantly today, her head bowed. Someone in the audience at a lecture series sits ramrod straight with her arms tightly crossed at her chest, indicating a "Doubting Thomas" attitude. I know a very potent therapist whose mode of listening includes sitting in the identical posture as his client. He tells me he finds connection easier by matching his body language with the client's, that it opens a wider channel for discovery.

I grew up in an era where body language often told a different story from verbal communication, belying what was really going on. There were cultural mores against talking about anything sad or troubling; if you didn't voice a problem, it didn't exist. A person's individual truth was not talked about within the family or out in the world in my growing-up era.

As a culture I believe we are trying to become healthier, thank goodness. Many of us feel free to be honest and forthright with each other in order to be connected. I'm included in this group. This doesn't mean I go around spewing forth my truth to any and all. Natural discretion dictates to whom, where, and when I come forth. But it feels congruent to allow myself to be real in the world and to allow others to be equally authentic. Therefore, when I go forth each day, I need not confuse others by having a sign that is unreadable because it's upside down, untrue. In this way I am more easily connected to all.

Giving Up Our Separateness

Ram Dass says in his tape, "Conscious Ageing," that we get so focused on our separateness we lose unity with others.[2] That as long as we identify only with our separateness, we will fear death.

Growing up seemed all about competition, climbing up, looking "better than." I would bet that many of us were encouraged to feel different, special, and unique. In that striving, isolation was common, a feeling of being alone. When the measurement was about how it looked on the outside, inevitably I fell short and felt separate. Because it's a time of appearing confident, I wonder if the hollow echo of many teens might be, "There's nobody who feels like I do."

In middle age now, I'm increasingly aware of the fallacy of this early training. Separateness kept me stalled, anxious about performance, and guilty for time spent doing my things—reading and dreaming. The false prize of "looking good" proved to be made of tin, not gold.

Whenever I failed, I felt alone, separate. But it was actually in failing that I learned. During the raising of my own family I found myself wanting in many areas, afraid my parenting skills weren't adequate. When my teenagers ran into perplexing problems, I felt alone, as if no one else faced these situations, because nobody talked about these things. The culture then mandated: Don't talk about anything unpleasant. When I realized that others before me had felt the identical confusion, I saw that I was part of humanity. What a burden was lifted when I discovered I was not better than, or worse than, other human beings. Finally I could drop the illusion that somehow I was special, due entitlements that others less fortunate had no claim to. I could quit climbing the impossible upward stretch of ladders that seemed to disappear into the clouds above.

A wise friend often advised me, "Wherever you are, be there." And I would add, "And it is all right to be there." It's very comforting to real-

---

2.   Ram Dass, *Conscious Aging* (Boulder, Colorado, Sounds True Recordings, 1992, series of two tapes)

ize that most likely we're all exactly where we should be on our journey, and that on our road we will not be alone but will be inextricably linked with others on their paths.

We will walk with them; sometimes passing them, sometimes lagging behind, and it's all good, despite appearances or what our minds tell us about our position on the path. Each human being is confronting roadblocks at different times; we're all striving for balance, for a sense of purpose.

The outcomes of our journeys will be as different as individual fingerprints. But underneath it all lays the thread of community with others, a grasping onto likeness. A feeling of, "I am not alone," permeates the human pathways when we symbolically join hands with others.

So, how did I get to my core, become who I am, learn to be authentic? It was a slow process and became what I now call "An Inside Job."

5

Authenticity—an Inside Job

Appreciation Time

When my anxious hat pops on my head, it's usually accompanied by thoughts that I am somehow of less value than others. At these times I need to remember that everything is all right at this moment. There's nothing I'm doing or thinking that's deliberately hurtful to others. And I usually see that there's nothing I ought to be rushing about doing.

I'm still learning to fully trust myself. I know now that when I look to others for validation, expecting them to hold answers for me, an illusion has taken charge. This illusion tells me others are more intelligent and hold the keys to my life's doors. But this is simply not so.

Everything I've experienced fills in the picture of who I am today. It's like knitting with yarn that is a blend of colors. I can't separate the threads; I must use the blend for my finished product. My completed work will be individual, no other like it anywhere. It is mine with my past and present intertwined. And this product of mine is as well knitted as others', holding value of its own.

I am not merely here to pass the time. I need to recognize that there's a reason, a purpose to my life, and it can become an exciting adventure to explore that purpose. There will be teachers, every day, if I am looking, listening, open and willing.

As a human being maneuvering through the labyrinth of life, I have my own filter. Others could interpret the same set of circumstances differently. However I arrive at decisions, if the fit makes sense and feels comfortable, most likely it's the correct response for my individual life. Outer reality will always be filtered through my own experience and shouldn't be classified as right or wrong, good or bad. Many times it's a blend.

When I begin to judge myself, hearing a critical voice, I question the judge—and, by the way, I'm the judge. I ask for clarification. I ask myself, "Will these actions harm me or others?" I run my conclusions through a sieve of honesty. Am I being selfish and self serving? Or, am I truly caring about others?

A lot of times I use calm, supportive comments to myself. This is not to say that I can't correct myself or reverse my course of action. But once my decisions have passed the truth test and no residual discomfort remains in my body, I can proceed with assurance that, for me, this is the right path. I can tell by the ease of my breathing. There is no tightness or constriction.

In her book, *Codependent No More*, Melody Beattie says, "We are the greatest thing that will ever happen to us. Believe it. It makes life much easier." [1] When I trust myself, I relax and stay in today. I take off my anxious hat.

---

1.   Melody Beattie, *Codependent No More* (Center City, Minnesota, HarperColllins Publishers, A Hazelden Book, 1987)

Looking Is Not Necessarily Seeing

One evening I was listening to the most beautiful music. Pure, clear tones rang out with such clarity. They resonated deep inside of me. It was the voice of Andrea Bocelli. I learned he is blind. Why should that surprise me? Such a powerful voice this man has! Without thought, I had assumed sight necessary to his astounding ability.

This is a man whose eyes cannot look, but as he himself says, "I can see." Perhaps he can see to a finer degree than most sighted people; he can see visual imagery with exquisite sensitivity. And with this vision, unbridled beauty is released.

I close my eyes trying to experience what this no-sight would be like. As I listen to his voice with my eyes open and then with my eyes closed, there *is* a difference. With closed eyes there's a special radiance about his voice. Somehow it is richer with sight closed off. And with my eyes closed, without distraction, I am forced deep inside.

Almost everything in the world seems to be experienced on the outside. But the richness is increased, the sensitivity sharpened, when focus occurs from inside the heart and soul. Great poets, writers, and musicians roll out their beauty and wisdom from the inside. The heart takes over where vision stops. It seems to me that creativity has little, if anything, to do with the thinking brain. Letting go of thoughts, releasing mental activity, opens the door, and creativity flows, naturally, without strain.

We don't talk about it much—this ability to perceive. For many years I looked but did not see. It wasn't until darkness descended upon me that I finally emerged with sight. I had spent too much time beholding emptiness, sedating my senses. When I finally woke up, I saw the brilliant colors of sunsets, of rainbows, with such clarity that it startled me. Seeing from deep inside helped me live authentically. It was like taking off dark glasses. I bless that day.

Fishing

Different species of fish reside in different bodies of water. One wouldn't expect to find a swordfish in a mountain stream. Nor could a rainbow trout be caught off the coast of Florida.

But isn't that what I do all the time with the people in my life? I put my line in the water day after day with some hope, some expectation of the people I interact with, only to be surprised and disappointed when what I get is not what I expected. I fish daily and am surprised when what bites the line doesn't have the traits or characteristics I anticipated.

Some people go fishing daily for a *Father-Knows-Best* kind of dad and end up with Pat Conroy's rigid, militaristic father in his book, *The Great Santini*. A line is dropped into a liberal tank with the expectation of a conservative catch. Or I put a hook out for sensitivity and come up empty. "She just doesn't get it," I say. The problem is, it is *I* who doesn't get it! I'm stuck like a damaged music CD. Same bait, same spot, same expectation, same result. This is the denial trap—my refusal to see a person or situation as it is. "I know what I'm looking for and this is the pond in which it will be found," I insist. I keep looking for some impossible ideal, superimposing an image I've selected over an actual situation or person.

Some fishermen, not finding that which they expect, give up and bitterly vow never to fish again. But the pull is strong so I do a turnabout and return to the same spot, expecting the same unreal outcome. I become jaded. This kind of stubborn persistence and insistence can ultimately turn on me, preventing me from accepting reality.

And what about the fish? How must it feel to be caught and struggle to the surface only to see a frown and a disappointed look. I have a vision of their frustration to never measure up to the expectation of the fisherman.

A breakthrough from this frustration came for me through a prayer, "Father, let me see this situation, this person as you see this situation, this person. Open my eyes, change my response as I seem unable to do this myself."

At times I have to become exceedingly uncomfortable before I remember to ask for help. When I do this, God helps me understand that I am to let go and relax into what is. I fish for different understandings. I change my attachment to fishing outcomes, trying to welcome what's there as it is, nothing more. I start with acceptance. Only then do I find peace with my fish!

Family Rules

RULE NUMBER ONE:
THOU SHALT PUT THY HAIR IN THY MOTHER'S HANDS.

Mother was in charge of my hair when I was growing up. Every morning I stood before her dresser mirror while she fussed, combed, pulled and parted my hair. I suffered horrible smelling perms at an early age, and every picture of me reveals barrettes, combs, and monstrous bows in my hair. I had no choice in the matter.

RULE NUMBER TWO:
THOU SHALT NOT BE FRIGHTENED.

When I was six years old, I could not sleep and came downstairs to the living room where my parents were entertaining friends. "I'm scared," I said. "No, you're not, honey," my mother told me. "Now go on back to bed." As I climbed the stairs I thought to myself, "I could have sworn I was scared." I first identified with this dilemma in a lecture by John Bradshaw.

RULE NUMBER THREE:
THOU SHALT NOT BE ANGRY.

The only one in our home who was allowed the privilege of anger was my father. The Vice President of a natural gas company, he was frequently called after hours with gas line emergencies. He would receive calls in the middle of supper, and from the hallway telephone, one could hear the loud, "Oh, damn!" He'd say, "I'm on my way," slamming the phone down and grabbing his coat. We could hear the hasty exit from the driveway. My dad was called "the gray fox" because he drove a gray Lincoln and he always arrived at the broken-line site in record time. Especially in business matters, anger seemed a powerful fuel for my father. The rest of us mostly stayed on the easy side, and I behaved as I was expected to behave—like a "lady."

RULE NUMBER FOUR:
THOU SHALT NOT ARGUE WITH THE HEAD OF THE HOUSE.

My grandmother was a Democrat, my father a staunch Republican. Sunday dinners were full of suspense as inevitably the conversation turned to what Roosevelt was doing now. I held my breath. One did not challenge my father; but bless her, my sweet natured little grandmother would quietly defend her President. In a placid, gentle voice she simply held her ground through the dinner, and her son would finally stop the conversation with a suggestion that we all go for a ride in the car, which always ended up right at her house—good-bye, Nana.

RULE NUMBER FIVE:
THE BREAST OF THE CHICKEN IS RESERVED FOR THE HEAD OF THE HOUSE.

Every Sunday we had fried chicken for dinner, and when asked which piece I would like, mother's fork poised over the leg or thigh as she raised her eyebrow. I loved it when my father was out of town on business for the sole reason that I could have the breast of the chicken! I was in my teens before I realized that women could be deserving of this choice piece also.

RULE NUMBER SIX:
THE IMAGE OF THE PERFECT FAMILY SHALT BE MAINTAINED AT ALL TIMES.

I was told early on that things going on in the family must remain in the family. We looked good in the neighborhood, looked good at school, in the community, and at church. At times there was a dichotomy that felt unreal. I would be sad or mad, but felt required to maintain the smile. I had a limited vocabulary for words that describe feelings, not learning how to identify these emotions until much later in life. I came to understand that feelings translate into thoughts, which translate into actions.

TODAY'S RULE:
BE TRUE TO THYSELF.

Ultimately, I learned that what was *more* important than rules was authenticity. Matching my insides with how I present myself on the outside has been a lifelong process. Today, I will not trade my congruent, real self for any worn out, useless rule.

The Right Port

Who manages my money market fund? Not me. Who manages my grocery store? Not me. Who manages the building I live in? Again, not me. There must be something I'm in charge of. Oh yes, I'm in charge of me.

I am in charge of steering my ship of life into the port of my choice. At some landings the water appears smooth. Other places rough and dangerous. It can be a port of gaiety—a frivolous port. Or it can be one of quiet waters and contemplation. Many possible ports of entry appear throughout life. Some are entered with ease; others present challenges.

At times in my youth it was the follow-the-crowd port. I did what everyone did—joined the applauding crowd in the busiest cove. Some who voyaged there with me got stuck in this port, never to leave.

The mystique of muddy water ports called me at times. Some ports offered an experience that belied the surface. They appeared calm and serene from the top, but below beckoned a deep undercurrent that could have swept me up and out, never to return.

I am responsible for deciding which port I enter and how long I stay. As I live longer, I learn which places offer safety, which spots comfort me, which sites suit me. I become better at gauging the waters that are just the right temperature, the ideal depth. It might not be the place where many boats are docked, perhaps no more than a few. But instinct tells me, "This is the place."

When I learn that my life does not need to fit a mold or be a parody of lives around me, then and only then am I able to say, "I have found my place." I am free to pursue and investigate this port to my heart's content. I am also free now to help those stranded in near-by deep waters. Help them disentangle from the weeds and perhaps find the port of their own safety and comfort. I've found my port; can I help you find yours?

Body Lessons

A friend shared a quote from the famous philosopher, Norman O. Brown. "What is always speaking silently is the body. Listen to it." This quote reached out to me. For so many years I was not aware of nor did I pay much attention to my body. I never wondered at its miraculous precision. It was simply an instrument to carry out my wishes.

As always, hindsight is perfect, and I now can look back and spot the times when my body was subtly trying to give me directions. For instance, our bodies tell us that certain people are toxic to us, we feel sick or tense or anxious, while others fill us with pleasure just by being around them.

At times growing up, there were fierce arguments between my mother and my brother. I would sit in my closet with my bears and my books trying to dull the commotion. After their explosions, fear robbed me of my appetite.

Once during my pre-puberty years, I was an unintended witness to sudden tragedy. Although a horrific event, I didn't seem to be terribly affected. It seemed my emotions just "shut down." I went into neutral, my feelings flattening out. My emotions were on hold, and this was no doubt a protection. But this protection too long held turned into a general denial system that in the long run became detrimental. During later years I would circumvent pain by shutting down. But after too many years of closing down emotion, my body began pushing me to wake up. The unresolved grief pushed against my lungs and stomach, shoving me towards acknowledgment. Three different occasions of viral pneumonia, and a stomach ulcer flashed warning signals. Sudden crying spells came out of nowhere, for no reason. I was confused by this physical rebellion.

Finally, finally I began looking at how my inner life might be creating the outward physical misery. I learned that stifled, stuffed pain does not go away, does not disappear. On the contrary, it stays inside, growing larger like moistened yeast, and it slowly turns poisonous—the poison being released into the body. With encouragement and guidance, I forged into the pain of the past and learned how to identify it. "Lean into the pain to come through it," was the wise advice. When I finally and authentically dealt with pain, when I let the healing tears fall, it was like taking my heart out of the freezer, allowing it to melt, to feel once again.

There was a noticeable improvement in not only my mind and emotions, but in my body. A new lightness flourished. I made the decision to face and deal with new pain instead of shut down or run away. I became aware that there was a capacity for joy that I had not experienced before. Laugher bubbled up from deep within. My eyes viewed the world with fresh delight.

My stomach is my barometer these days. I know that when my stomach feels tight and hurts, when I can't breathe deeply, my body is telling me to take a look at what is going on inside.

My body is my friend today and if I will but pay attention, it will lead me into health every time.

Finding the Fire Inside

In the movie *Adaptation,* a man tells his twin brother, "It's what you love, not what loves you that's important."[2] While it seems as if "who" rather than "what" would be the correct word, I think "what" hits the mark.

Isn't the brother saying that a person's drive towards that which he instinctually loves is crucially important? That over and above the directions of others, what we are passionate about is what counts.

In a creative writing class I facilitate, I instructed the class to write a short piece describing what they are passionate about. I told them it could be a person, place, or thing—whatever stirs enthusiasm. Wisdom lies in the belief that whatever your hand turns to naturally is the thing to pursue. One of my passions is writing and that passion pulls out the stopper and pours out thoughts and ideas like warm syrup. One has only to begin. I watched light bulbs turn on in the students' heads. That one exercise produced strong pieces of work.

Another idea from *Adaptation* that spoke to me indicated that one must adjust in order to thrive in the world. It's not enough to have passion. We must also be able to adapt when necessary. Otherwise, we would go racing around in self-will, blocking other people's paths. Pursuing our passion must be tempered with observation about the needs of those surrounding us. Otherwise, the gift of our passion can swiftly evolve into arrogance, allowing our ego to place us above others.

There is a natural timing for the surfacing of passion. Usually we know our proficiencies. But we can be waylaid. The persuasion of important figures in our lives—teachers, parents, and friends—may thwart us. It takes time and maturity to recognize our true path.

Mistakes are often assumed to be negatives to be avoided at any cost. Yet I have learned as much from mistakes as I have from successes. The refuse of mistakes has prodded me to ascend to higher levels of understanding. The intuitive part of me that mistakes call into awareness can

---

2.   Charles Kaufman, *Adaptation,* (Columbine Tri-Star, 20003)

act as a guide, alerting me that trying to push events against an apparent tide of resistance may not be the way to accomplish my goal.

I know from inside what turns on the lights for me. I know what thoughts and ideas draw me in close. I am acutely aware of those ideals that linger and recur. And there is an important color scheme to follow. Some ideas are exciting and thrilling but carry the warning color of red—although a magnet draws me, wisdom cautions. Others might travel that particular road with impunity, but through wrong turns of the past, I have learned which paths are safe for me. Other opportunities carry an obvious green light, an immediate okay to proceed down that path. I learn which passion to indulge and which to avoid.

When at last I have settled on that which rings a bell for me, the next step is perseverance—steadfastness, constancy, and persistence.

The writing desire, which I have always had, pushes ahead of me clearing the way like a leaf blower clearing the sidewalk. The experience of watching where my fingers take me satisfies and excites me. Sentences flow effortlessly, and just when I think my ideas have all been expressed, a fresh page magically fills up. Like a lake, which goes dry with no input, my lake of imagination fills up from streams of thought, born from life experiences.

I shall always have something to do, even when my limbs and sight slide into imperfection in later life. Passion becomes lasting joy, my own perfect fit.

Nice Girl

For most of my life, I've been called nice—nice girl, nice teacher, nice lady. The dictionary definition of "nice" includes: "fastidious, discriminating; marked by delicate discrimination or treatment; pleasing, agreeable." Also, "well-executed; well bred; virtuous; respectable." Then we start going downhill: "choosy, finicky, particular, persnickety" (that's a dictionary word?) "prudish." And surprisingly: "foolish, wanton, ignorant." So many words of description for only four letters of the alphabet.

Something rankles me, bores me stiff about the bestowed complement of nice. At its very sound, I picture a blank canvas, innocuous, vacuous.

Would I rather be called good? At least that word is defined in the dictionary as: "improvement, interest, service," qualities of character instead of personality. How about a person of veracity, which indicates, "truthfulness, frankness, candor, honesty and fidelity." I like frankness and candor. I'll take either over nice.

There is no doubt that I spent most of my young life endeavoring to please. In a household that presented surprises of mood from my mother, surprises that revolved around the alarming activity of my older brother during his teen years, it became my duty somehow to present the "sunny side" of the family. I shined at this. Having a natural base of optimism, it wasn't difficult. It became my mission to propel others into the belief that the world was fair, just, and that right would triumph in the end.

Listening to a lecture by John Bradshaw, who was my first teacher of self-forgiveness and love, a phrase he used resonated inside me. He talked about the "price of nice," and the price is one's self. Somewhere along my "pleasing" path through life, I'd lost myself. Like a flat brain wave, "nice" no longer served me. I woke up to find that I had little idea of what I wanted, and no idea of who I was.

However comfortable it remains to be always agreeable, something of value stays surrounded in mist when this mode of operation becomes the steersman of my life's boat. Pleasing everybody is myth, impossible to accomplish, and even if I could, there's something less than honest about it.

One day I saw that I was seeking to be a more authentic person. The outline of who I am became more defined. It *wasn't* that I ceased to be pleasant; it *wasn't* that I no longer was willing to accommodate others; it was that inside I had a clearinghouse of old ideas. "Whatever you want," disappeared from my vocabulary. At last I was able to formulate and identify from the inside a truer and more refined image of who I am. My outside behavior began to match my inside state.

It's not that life has become more about *I* and *Me*. It's about balance. It's that I can identify and claim my own ideas and voice them, work to reach compromises with others, and still hang onto my "niceness." I no longer have to mutter to myself a differing opinion, mentally criticizing another's ways. Somehow I'm thrown into neutral. I haven't elevated myself above others, nor am I subservient, remaining in a shy-dome world of my own. I can relate on an even basis, one human being to another. I am part of an exciting world, not separate in the world. I've lived a long life and I *do* have something to say. Today I'm a more authentic person.

Waking Up

Hello! Wake up—this is your life! Today, right this moment, this is my life. It isn't yesterday which is reflected with regret or joy; it isn't tomorrow, which may appear smoky and mysterious but also promise something better. Today, it's today in which my life appears. And it can be a beginning, a turning around, a different journey from yesterday's journey.

Yet it appears there's no room for today. It's like a pail, which is already full, full of yesterday's waste and yesterday's facts. No space for anything new.

Maybe it's time to empty my pail, just turn it upside down and empty its contents. What? I can't throw away all those carefully planned yesterdays, can't just ignore what has gone before. It would be a sacrilege.

While I am not aware of the exact origin of this quote, I was told by a friend that Ram Dass said that as children, we are given a space suit to wear, one which our parents construct for us. Rightly so. They naturally have to do this, as we are too young to know anything about taking care of ourselves. The space suit comes with directions that we follow as we grow up. As long as we are under our parents' roof, under their care, of necessity we have to wear the suit.

But eventually the space suit becomes uncomfortable, tight and constricting. We can't move around freely. We begin to think about things, use our experience—limited as it is—to imagine something different, something new for ourselves. Those space-suit rules, which at first seemed natural, now pinch like outgrown shoes.

Unfortunately, other people tend to freeze us as we were long ago. They don't want us to shed our space suits. It frightens them because they're used to seeing us a certain way. When we take off the suit, they have to readjust their perceptions. Changing anything can create discomfort.

Some of us live our whole lives in that original space suit. We sleep through opportunities to make life changes. We doze comfortably in the old. The illusion is, what once worked will always work. Some of us are jolted out of this sleep by life itself. We are forced to go inside with our flashlights and examine the dusty basements of our lives. There sit those full pails we spent our lives filling. We open that long-stuck door to fresh air and do a clean sweep.

It's a calling, this waking up. Somewhere deep within the soul, springs of fresh water begin bubbling up to the surface and we are powerless to stop the flow. It just comes.

The genuine inside search for a fit takes precedence over everything. This calling to our deeper self to me is God's grace. Out of the blue, when the old one does not serve us anymore, when we become willing to surrender our old suit for a new one, it's bestowed upon us.

And the day that I shed my old space suit was a blessed day.

It's All About Me

In one of his tapes, "Letting Go: A Spirituality of Subtraction," Father Richard Rohr infers that we don't meet anyone else. We keep meeting ourselves in different forms: our fears, angers, hurts, desires, and need to control are implanted in those with whom we come into contact.[3]

It seems a human condition that we put expectations on others that originate within our own life experiences. We put our own stuff out there onto other people. I believe this practice of planting my fear, hurts, and desires upon the person standing before me may be quite common. I know that often I receive not what really is, but that which I'm expecting. This reminds me of a story: A man is sitting by the side of the road. Another man comes by and asks, "Tell me, what is the next town like? I am headed there." The man at the side of the road asks, "Well, what was the town like that you just left?" The man replies, "Oh, they were stingy, distrustful, and selfish." The man then replied, "That's what you will find in the next town." Later on another man comes by and asks the fellow by the road the same question. Again the man replies with a question, "Tell me, what was the town like that you are from?" This man replied, "Well, they are wonderful people, kind, compassionate, loving." And again the answer, "That's what you will find in the next town."

Father Rohr says that he believes that most of the evil in the world is summed up in one word: ego. It seems I must be interrupted in my ego-driven life, be confronted with my powerlessness before I can surrender, give up my illusion of authority and control.

Evidently, I don't notice the ego's cunning manipulation until I'm confronted with a roadblock. Then when I can go no further on my path, I have a choice: I can either surrender and give up my illusion or I can fight and demand my entitlement, the right to do things my way. For example, I might insist there is only one school my child should

---

3.   Richard Rohr, O.F.M., *Letting Go: A Spirituality of Subtraction* (Cincinnati, Ohio, Saint Anthony Messenger Press, 1987, series of eight tapes)

attend when the roll is full and entrance is denied. I can continue to complain and push the situation or surrender to the fact that maybe this school is not the right choice at this time.

My ego will seek and find facts that support the thoughts that make me right. At times my mind is most assuredly the enemy of my well-being and peace. My mind by itself is a dangerous place because it leads me straight into ego. When I go in there alone without benefit of feed-back from others, I go with a flashlight and a gun! The ego voice says, "It's all about my image, my perspective, my needs."

Father Rohr says that our image of ourselves is what stands in our way to truth. And he says, "God has to torpedo that image to reach us." [4]

It was with great relief when I realized that the torpedo had reached me and removed me from my self-centered world—blew me out of the water of self-absorption. Like Jonah, I was ejected onto another land, one where I was gently taught what was real.

This grace of awareness about the damaging effect of ego was granted to me. The soil inside was being prepared by reactions to life and it took years to make this soil available for planting and reaping. When the soil of my soul was ready to turn itself over, to relinquish any and all control, then the miracle happened. Finally I was able to turn to others and God and say, "I don't understand. Please help me." My mind complied and ego retreated, for a while. But this priceless awareness has to be renewed daily. Ego has a way of sneaking quietly back to first base.

When I can say the above six simple words, they deliver me into a surprising and rewarding sense of serenity. It's all okay. A compassion-ate friend once told me long ago, "Everything everywhere is already all right." It has taken me years to come to an understanding of this phrase. It means that no matter what things are going on at the present, it is part of a total picture we may not understand until much

---

4. Richard Rohr, O.F.M. *Great Themes of Scripture*

later. Through the practice of getting out of my mind and ego and into reality, I stretch and find peace.

Who You Is and Who You Ain't

I wish I knew the author of the following, but I do not. "If you keep being who you ain't, you ain't never gonna be who you is."

How prophetic. I know I've spent significant time trying to be the person someone else wanted me to be. I developed an antenna acutely attuned to other people and their wishes. Intuition told me what they needed, and I tried to meet those needs. I grew up in a home where emotions were not discussed, and tension would build until the pitcher of everyone's feelings brimmed over. Most of my actions growing up were centered on pleasing others in order to dim the fire of tension.

The stage upon which my life plays out is a kaleidoscope of scenes. I can start out in one scene true for me in the morning, but by afternoon the scene has changed to one of your choosing. I lose my own scene to keep peace.

One day I became aware of the wide variety of reactions I am capable of, and I took stock to see which ones matched my insides and which did not. I found that evidently I could play many roles. To collect and merge all my roles, to present one true picture became my goal.

I also find that I am a naturally reactive person. Whatever I am feeling or thinking instantly registers upon my face. I cannot successfully pull off a practical joke. My intention is to reflect nothing on my face whatsoever until I've gathered the facts and quietly processed them, but for me this does not come naturally. I've been intrigued by television characters who show little emotion on their faces, people who can wait until the other character in the play has finished talking before they jump in and emote. Simon Baker, the actor who plays Nick Fallon in the show, "The Guardian," exhibits this to a remarkable degree. On this show Mr. Fallon, the guardian ad-litum for children who need legal help, may be receiving information that would blow the socks off me, but his calm demeanor exhibits no show of emotion. He is present. He listens. Me? I would need Botox® injections to be this expressionless.

So, this is my target: to become detached enough to maintain dependable equilibrium while remaining true to myself, to protect others and myself from an immediate reaction that might make them and me uncomfortable. And I say to myself, "Good luck!"

The Truth Shall Set You Free

That the truth shall set us free is a valid premise—the basis for learning, the foundation for education. The truth is seen as a golden nugget, a superior goal in life. Seek the truth always. Wisdom is promised from truth.

From that bottom line, there appears to be offshoots that are more difficult to define. Little dips in the continuity of pure truth. First of all, there is the question, whose truth? My truth can be different from yours, but no less valid. I look upon my world through my own optical lens. You observe the world from yours. Where I might see the color yellow, you might see the same color as gold. Slight differences, but we each claim our own color as "truth." The sum of my experiences in life colors my view.

Objective reasoning says there is but one truth to most scientific questions, and one truth certainly in math equations. History presents what we think of as truth. Facts emerge that are reality based. My condo building has 20 floors. That is a fact. I am a certain age. That is a fact. Educationally those facts give us concrete knowledge. But those are not the truths that necessarily "set us free."

The *free* part is subjective. What I define as the "ah-hah!" experience, an inner coming together of truth, releases me to the joy of discovery—the discovery of a truth that fits for me. We all have different puzzles to put together in life. A piece that has no place in my puzzle, may fit perfectly in yours.

There is one truth that does not set me free. The truth about *you* does not necessarily set me free. I regret that as a human being I judge what others claim as truth. And it does not matter if I am "right" about you, clearly seeing your motives, your faults, in declaring something as valid. This truth about you does nothing to set *me* free. In fact, it does just the opposite. It makes me uncomfortable, this needing to set you straight! A struggle follows. And soon, I am caught up in the trap of wanting you to change, do it as I see it. And this is a prison. I am not free as long as I am trying to change you. As my friend Paula says, "I quit trying to make the fir tree be a rose bush."

I don't know what the answer is, human nature being human nature. But I see the value in granting others the freedom to choose their own truth while granting myself that same permission. As the years pass, I move from connecting to authenticity and reality and move towards inner strength. I attempt to free my voice, open my throat and speak my heart

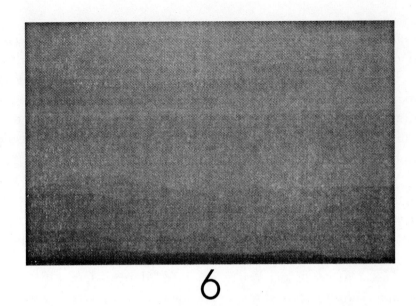

6

Ageing—Finding My Voice

Illusion of Ageing

I'm looking at my geraniums pleading for water, saying to myself, "Who cares. There's nobody to see them." My patio furniture needs cleaning, and again I say, "Who cares?" So I thought when I was a new widow growing older alone. I remember the malaise that permeated that day, the absent energy so available in earlier times. I knew this attitude opened the door to self-pity, a worthless emotion that feeds on itself, a snake twining itself around my mind.

The fear that my life has no meaning resurfaces at such times. When this mood settles like a cloak, I ask questions of myself: "What do you mean, 'Who cares?' Is my life over? Do I just give up now? Sit in a corner? The geraniums are for *me* and I matter. There are goals yet for me to make this shaky world a bit better; smile at a child, make conversation with a lonely neighbor." "Yeah, yeah! Big deal!" I answer myself.

It usually comes down to looking at which illusion I'm living in today. When I'm in the pits and wonder why, I'm usually accepting as truth a particular illusion about myself, someone else, or situation that I'm in. And the major illusion that still surfaces: I'm all alone in the world and I don't count.

With ageing, the illusion comes that it's almost over and I've not done important things. I haven't become the doctor I once envisioned, or written the great novel that's rattled around in my head, never finding its way to paper. I was unable to derail the inevitable from happening to my children.

"Just a darn minute! You're not God," I remind myself. "Your accomplishments are the bread of life, the small gentle acts of kindness, gestures of compassion that ease the paths of others. Without that thread running through a life, even glittering accomplishments lose their luster."

I may not have had a large spotlight to shine over a city, but a life well lived is made up of small flashlight beams that we shine for one another to light the way, open up the path for ourselves and others. Life is made up of the small steps up the steep hill, not the big leaps over mountains by fairy tale giants.

My illusion is that I haven't made a difference, that I don't count. But I've come to see that my life is not less important, nor more so than other lives. My life is simply a life, one light that hopefully shines long after I am gone through my children, grandchildren, and friends. I matter and I do make a difference. And so do my geraniums.

Gentle World

Sometimes at the delicate age at which I'm surprised to find myself, I feel like yelling, shouting to the frantic, loud, brash world, "Stop!" Stop this deranged pace, stop the rushing and pushing to be first. Where's the peace? Where did "Take all the time you need," go? What happened to courtesy and good manners, the "Thank you," and, "If you would, please?" Where did they go? Did they ever exist? Have things speeded up to an unbearable pace for anyone else, or is it just I?

As I look at the world right now it seems it's gone mad! War and evil abounds, people we trusted with our money have been cheating us, and the house of cards exists everywhere I look.

A measure of honesty and gentleness with each other, oneself, the community, and the world at large. That's what I want. Why can't we have that? And when will I take off my own judge's robe—grant others the measure of compassion I claim is so necessary, extend gentleness so lacking in the world.

I crave safety. Ever since I was a little girl I've trusted and believed what others told me, and bam! been astounded at malevolent intent. When I trust, only to be disappointed in people's veracity, it slowly empties my well of hope. But still I'm naïve—the good news and the bad. My baseline returns perennially to assume best intentions from others. It's easier for me to live this way.

Chronologically, I'm on the "downside of the mountain," and the innate desire for security, anywhere, anywhere at all, mounts daily. I *so* desire a community of kindness and mercy. So I ask myself, "What can I do about it?"

Loss of trust in the world, as with any loss, first erupts in anger. Yes, good old bag-punching anger! But I'm not much for marching city streets. Instead, I use my fingers and my voice. I pop out my beliefs on paper. I mail letters to individuals and to institutions. Today I am better equipped to deal with unfairness.

On this side of the mountain, I find that under anger, understanding can emerge, acceptance of reality. What is, is. Things are as they are. Finally, finally I come to surrender. Okay, I say, so there is evil. Vicious crimes exist. Unfairness abounds. I can't change the world. But I am not powerless. I am in control of myself, of my actions, attitude, and my response to life. I can seek peace then, individually, in my tiny segment of the world. Therein I have the gentleness and peace I crave. I create my own world—the reward of ageing.

So?

I'm tired. Tired of stewing and reacting over the small stuff. Like a balloon that has been inflated too many times, the fact that I'm ageing has taken the air out of reacting. It's too much trouble nowadays. This is the culmination of a life-long process within me to produce response, not reaction.

Pause. Wait. When my mind races with the, "What if this or that happens," I say a simple, "So? What's the worse that could happen in this situation? So what if all the movies in my head come true. So what?"

One of my less-pleasant pastimes has been to worry about the weather. "What if it rains? Rain will spoil the outdoor picnic, party, much of my day." If I have airplane trips planned, weather becomes a big issue. I love to fly, have taken flying lessons myself. But being in the air in a hefty storm frightens me. As a child, I worried about bad weather when I knew my father was flying home from a business trip.

Time has mediated my worrying patterns. Life is too short to waste time fussing. I'm better now saying, "So?" Part of me still says, "So, this is a big deal!" But I've learned to answer, "Oh, let it rain, will you?" That's growth!

Punctuation Marks of My Life

Commas:

My childhood years, where everything felt safe. My fresh eyes looked upon what seemed a steady, *reliable* world. My teen years, where I timidly ventured forth to experience the new. My college years, where each corner turned revealed exciting experiences—where slowly I tested the cities of life, and there was always another comma, more to be revealed.

Periods:

A time when my choices felt comfortably set in cement. My academic choices, my commitment to studies and a degree. My experimentation in the work world where I found my easy place as part of the machinery of a medical school. My choice of a mate and the follow-through to the extraordinary and fateful blending of two lives. The massive responsibility of raising a family, commitment to children. These periods in my lifeline seemed to be lined up for permanency. The course set upon seemed deliberate, fixed. Life appeared to be a continuous straight line to success and happiness. I foresaw no problems. I believed change would not alter these courses.

Exclamation Points:

The birth of four children. Miracle upon miracle emerged. As I embraced each tiny bundle of joy, I depended upon the always-reliable stability. Again, the line across the page of life stretched out indefinitely, straight and true.

The building of a home, a life, in which the steps seemed low and easy to manage. Paragraph after paragraph in the story line appeared in expected order. All exclamation points in this line were above the water level, seemingly out of reach from storms. Unfortunately and inevitably, however, the storms arrived. They flooded over the careful boundaries I'd erected. Sometimes gradually, sometimes with sudden, swift force, the predictability of life was washed away. Now the exclamation marks in my lifeline were bold in their interruption and black in color. Gone were the comforts of carefully spaced commas, periods, and exclamation marks, and in their place stood...

Question marks:

What happened? Where did the well-planned-for safety and security go? Why? Why did the carefully constructed developments go awry? Why was I not prepared, not notified ahead of the drastic changes? Why could I suddenly make no sense of the earthquakes rocking my life?

How? How could I fit the pieces of my life puzzle back together? How was I to proceed on my game plan of life? How to take all these seeming errors and correct them, force them to make sense again?

Who? Who was the weak link, the cause? Was it that person? This person? Was it I? Or was it powerful forces unknown and unforeseen? Who was going to help me get my bearings? Who was going to be the guide, now that I no longer seemed to have the map, now that the foundation of choice I thought I possessed collapsed.

So now I turn to a new page in my lifeline, one that is blank. Perhaps I can start over with the commas of life where there is more to be revealed. There's a fine line between fear and excitement. I'd like to choose excitement!

Snapshots of Life

When I take my film to be processed I have to choose the size: three-by-five, five-by-seven, or full panoramic. I like to compare my photographs with my inner vision that changes as the years pass.

Looking at the snapshots I took throughout my life, I see the different focus according to my age at the time. When I was a child, my sight was focused on the near, the local. There's Rusty, our dog. Nana is picnicking with us by a lake, and there's my dad watching my brother build something in the back yard.

Teen and college years delivered photos of greater scope, groupings of friends, outings on the lake, parties in the back yard. While the circle of life began to include the many, still it was confined to my small world.

In young adulthood the focus widened, like ordering five-by-seven pictures—family, pictures of my babies, and new homes, trips taken. There's the gaily-colored piñata for my daughter's birthday and my son in his little league outfit. In reviewing these photos, again I see the near, the local, only our own little world. To me, this little world was everything.

In my senior life, I buy panoramic film and the view broadens. And internally, now I can see the broad view from where I began to where I am now. I can see where clouds darkened the landscape in places—dark storm clouds, so dark that the view is obscured. But there are bright scenes with every detail visible. My internal camera in the last phase of life records with a wide eye, both my photos and my awareness.

Like looking down from above on the complete picture, valleys and peaks, rivers and seas are revealed. The mountains of West Texas from my beginnings shift to the flatlands of the Gulf Coast and back again to the mountains, further west. The snapshots depict my children now grown, and a beautiful new generation appearing—the progression and steady march of time evident in my grandchildren.

Oh, the colors in this panoramic view. Early photos were black and white, and then turned to muted blues to bright reds, yellow, and greens. I am grateful that this beauty continues unfolding. There seems no end to this breathless view. Although I am not in control of how long my life will be, I can determine its width and depth. My inner life has a perspective that was absent in my youth, the picture clearer now.

To an unseen Higher Presence, what a beautiful sight we must make on our journey through life. What a presentation to our Maker, each journey a unique blend.

I'm Not Done Yet

I'm in the 60's plus, but still the sun shines. There are things I've not accomplished yet, but I believe that many of them are still possible.

I'm thinking about finishing my flying lessons. At one time in my early twenties I wanted to be a flight attendant, but my father was adamant that I not undertake this risk. Some forty years later, in 1991, one year after my second's husband's death, I called an instructor, drove out to a small local airport and took my first flying lesson. Nothing can describe the feeling I had sitting in the tiny cockpit at the controls. Flying the small plane myself was an exhilarating experience! When I was given permission to take off, the ensuing emotional rush thrilled me. As the little Cessna charged down the runway, the suspense built, and finally, at the right speed, I pulled back and we took off like a kite in the wind.

I was to begin landing lessons when my son took his life. Everything in my life was drowned in a sea of grief. I never returned to the airport. My emotional wings were flattened—I was grounded. But now, years later, I'm thinking of going back to finish. It's time. I want to learn how to land. Like looking at a puzzle with one missing piece, I want to fill in that blank.

I want to let my experience of recovery from the death of loved ones serve others in some way. I want to be a beacon of light in the dark journey through grief. It's never too late to offer hope and strength to another.

It's never too late to continue learning and studying, anything and everything. There's still time to allow myself to read for hours, yes, even in the daytime. Why was that not permissible when I was growing up? The work ethic, I suppose. One should be productive and reading was a luxury. Now I allow myself this small pleasure anywhere and anytime.

I can still write a book. I've long wanted to write down the thoughts that gather in my mind each day, the small miracles I see on my walks in the park. I'd like to record bits of wisdom garnered through the years, record victories and losses with what I learned about the acceptance and calmness that comes from simply doing the next thing without losing hope. I'd like to be someone my grandchildren can come to with need for comfort when confronted with the inevitable hardness of life.

Although I know it is not possible in any direct way, somehow I would like to pass on to my grandchildren my faith in God. Their lives are brimming with people and activities, information bombarding them every hour, every day. But there will come a time when life's tornadoes, large or small, will level their ground, and they will need inner strength, the certainty of a loving unseen presence, that I believe under girds life. I'd like them to know that there is an organized unfolding in this world, a coherence (even though it appears not to be so), that there is a reliable force of benevolent value, of unconditional love beyond our own consciousness, and that we all belong to something infinite and good beyond our imagination.

All in all, there are a multitude of tasks left for me to accomplish. Perhaps that is why I am still here.

If I Had It To Do Over

I am a member of what is called, "The Silent Generation," those raised around the time of the Second World War. The culture of that time did not encourage women to believe in themselves. We usually deferred to the male, which had an upside—we were relieved of decision-making.

But, if I had it to do over, I would trust myself more. In my family deferring to my dad was a natural: he was smart, good looking, and magnetic. But many times I intuitively believed I had a solution, and as things turned out I was right, but I didn't speak up. In my home one did not question parents, especially my father. That's just the way it was.

If I had it to do over, I would say more. I had a lifetime of "not saying." Not saying what was in my heart, what I disagreed with, how I felt. A do-over would mean I would voice my opinion more. I would allow myself to take a stand earlier in life. And I would sing, too—out loud, with confidence!

If I had it to do over, I would follow my instincts and my dreams. Pressures to conform would not deter me. I would allow myself the full freedom of creative expression. I would write with abandon.

I would pick my college major by my interest and laugh at those of the '50's who proposed that the sanctioned options for girls at college were education, nursing, and secretarial training. If I'd followed my heart, today I'd be in the medical field or journalism.

If I had it to do over, I would live for a while in a convent. No, that can't be right! Where did that come from? But it's true; I did indeed at times envision myself in the company of those who shared my simple belief in a benevolent God. At tumultuous times in my family of origin, the serenity of a quiet, cloistered existence presented an attractive possibility.

If I had it to do over, I would laugh, cry, and shout if I felt like it, with unbridled enthusiasm. I wouldn't care a fig what the neighbors thought. As long as I did no harm to others or myself, I would free myself to live vigorously. I would *not* be a perfect lady at all times; I would be as free as I was at seven when my brother and I ran bare-footed on the white sands of New Mexico, hooting and hollering to each other.

I would love more, risk more, laugh more, and above all, be *exactly* who I am with gusto—with pride! Other than that, I'd make the same mistakes but recover with a bit more grace.

Having discovered my truth and my voice didn't necessarily make life easy. There were mountains yet to climb and bone crushing loss materialized in many shapes and forms. At times situations waylaid the process of recovery from loss, urging me to get stuck in grief, mired in the valley of misery.

In the next chapter are the routes I sought to restore my heart and mind.

7

Melting Frozen Grief

Level of Vision

As I walk in the park every morning I've noticed that my sight has gradually shifted. It's no longer fixed on the path, the next step before me. When my daughter decided to end her life of despair three years after her brother made the same choice, I walked for my sanity. At the time, walking in the park relieved my torment. But then, my sight was on the ground.

Back then, I would find myself holding my breath. Slowly I began to breathe fully again. At first, big gulps when I remembered to breathe, when my chest would expand enough to receive the air. Then gradually I began to lift my head, and receive the merciful air deeper inside. I carried my Walkman, earpieces firmly in place. I couldn't stand the silence. So I listened to the news and talk shows. Music was too personal, too likely to trigger a field of emotion and tears. I felt I had to hold myself together—couldn't let go. The tears I had shed so far had not been enough for real relief.

One day I tried a favorite music station, and was awed when the first piece played was a song my daughter had left for me. She'd made a list of things to do, and last on the list had been, "Buy song for Mom—*Because You Loved Me*." The beautiful words flooded my being:

> You were my strength when I was weak,
> You were my voice when I couldn't speak.
> You were my eyes when I couldn't see,
> You saw the best there was in me.
> Lifted me up when I couldn't reach
> You gave me faith cause you believed.
> I'm everything I am because you loved me.
>
> Celine Dion[1]

Walls of protection against feeling melted away and my walking path blurred. Sitting on a bench hidden by the branches of a tree, I let the tears flow. To my relief, I didn't fall apart. I didn't descend into an abyss. I understood that it was okay. It was okay to let the tears cleanse the wound of loss. The tension melted, my shoulders relaxed, and my head lifted. The constriction in my chest lessened.

Grief had become something of a companion, but one I'd hoped to lose. Daily, the overwhelming need to connect just one more time with my children pushed against my heart. Now with the flow of tears, the losses blended. The tears unleashed the collected pain. There was total surrender this time. My prayers for comfort had been answered. A calm sense of everything being in place, exactly as it should be in God's

---

1. Celine Dion, *Because You Loved Me*, (Sony Music Entertainment, [Canada] Inc., 1996).

plan despite the circumstances, spread over my being. I did not have to ask why anymore, did not have to understand or have things explained. I accepted that at such harsh times there are no answers. And I felt peace that day.

The walks continued along with my prayers for strength. These walks and silent conversations with God seemed to be the only thing that delivered a sense of relief and comfort.

As the years passed, inch-by-inch, my line of vision changed. My sight climbed from the step ahead of me to the trunks of trees. The bark became the focus: the shades of gray, brown, and ivory of the different trees. Soon the grass and the lake appeared. Ducks swimming and geese skidding into a stop on the lake—people fishing by the side of the lake. I noticed children on their bikes and people skating, couples holding hands.

It's spring now, many years after my children's deaths. There's a lovely fragrance in the air, and I've observed purple irises holding their heads proudly above hearty red geraniums. Squirrels have approached offering the return of my smile.

Today my sight has lifted to the mountain peaks, and I see the brilliance of the blue Colorado sky. And with the raising of my sight, a lift of hope appears.

Grief—A Building Material

"WE CANNOT DIRECT THE WIND,
BUT WE CAN ADJUST THE SAILS."

This quote was found on a greeting card and unfortunately, the author was not named.

If caught in a storm on a lake in a sailboat, I cannot direct the wind. But I can adjust the sails of the boat to keep from capsizing. This thought has reminded me that in life I don't have to drown in times of adversity. My deepest wounds can become my greatest strengths.

I recall a vivid dream I had after my husband died. I was in a turbulent sea on a sailboat. Climbing up to adjust the sails, I was talking to my friend who was standing below watching me. When I reached the adjustment line, I looked down on deck. There was no one there. I looked out to sea and saw the great expanse of water. I was alone. In the dream I knew if I were to survive, it was up to me.

Life is so fragile. Like lightening, we can be struck down by accident in an instant. The storms of life present opportunity to face truth. After I manage to reach land in my sailboat, I'm handed reality, my particular piece of earth at this time. The need is to use the clay I've been handed to construct shelter. I can either accept it, or in disgust throw it away and sit on my hands in grief. The tent of self-pity is large. But I can refuse to sit there.

In my own case it took inner work, hard work. I looked at a picture of an adobe house in the southwest and likened the making of those bricks to my journey. After life's blows, my wounds became my own mound of raw dirt and clay. My job, if I chose, was to transform it into sturdy, strong bricks with which to build a new life. I could sit in silent resentfulness with this mound, this burden, or I could begin to work. I gave myself time, treated myself gently, and asked only for that which I was capable of doing that day. And I kept the target of creation in view.

To my particular raw dirt of circumstances I added the water of my tears. The moisture was necessary to handle the dirt, the pain, to form it. The strength and courage does not magically appear. I worked for it.

I am able to do a lot. All by myself I can strive to change my attitudes, move to improve my insight and belief system. I can turn my skills into something positive with which to work my clay. But I need a blueprint and that, for me, is given to me by something much more than my finite mind can come up with.

That plan, that blueprint, is in God's hands. He appears in the soil of vulnerability and surrender. He alone knows just what this formula is and what to do with the result. I can stumble along, fumbling my way, guessing the right mix, or I can ask for guidance in turning my pain into something of worth. I ask.. I give up my ego and turn to my source. The asking always results in answers—the exact mix for my particular pain. The results are amazing, the dirt and clay form something of surprising beauty that I could never have thought of alone. I'm given the blueprint to build something of true value.

Nature's Answers to Death

Nature abounds with answers to my questions about life and death. I think about my beloved mountains. Those mountains were there yesterday. They are here today. They will be here tomorrow. Supporting my faith, deep in nature, I observe wonders and miracles that verify the idea of the continuity of the human soul.

In our lives with loved ones, we usually consider that our relationship will be permanent. We think we have all the time in the world to be with someone, to show them how much they mean to us. But none of us knows when we will leave, or when our loved ones must leave us. We are not given tickets that read, "One life until 85 years of age." Like shells on a beach, some of us will be washed back into the place from which we came before others. We cannot know when that call will come.

To lose a loved one is searingly painful. When it happened to me, it was as if the world stopped. Indeed, my life with that person had ended. I felt lost, as if I would not be able to navigate, find my way without that person in my life. When the numbness wore off, I felt the pain of loss so deeply it often made the simple act of breathing arduous. I thought, "I can not endure this again. I won't live if I have to feel this pain again."

But I did endure this pain again—as most of us do. Eventually, I realized that if I looked upon death as some strange aberration that appeared out of the blue to attack me personally, a monster who robbed me of my loved ones, I would not recover. I refused to become bitter, consumed by self-pity.

For me, this acceptance that death is part of life was crucial to my recovery. I was not turning my loved ones over to nothingness—conscripting their souls to the darkness of nonexistence. I believe the spirit, the soul, cannot perish, does not die. To me, these loved ones are going through a natural, inevitable passage of this thing we call life. Who can say it might not be the very best stage of life?

I am fortunate to have a firm belief in God and his grace. I am a Christian, and the most comfort I have today is knowing in my innermost being that a loving, benevolent God is in charge and he has not taken my loved ones—he has received them.

I know that someday the shells of my life—beloved family members and friends—will wash away to sea again. Some loved ones will disappear singly; others seem to follow right on top of one another. I choose to believe that this part of life is probably the most unbelievably peaceful and joyful experience possible that we can in no way fathom, we who are left here on earth...not yet. I see affirmation of the soul's continuity in the mountains and in the shells, in nature that surrounds me.

Springtime

Springtime in the Rockies, and the beauty of the awakening earth startles me. As I walk in the park early this morning, the surprise of new blossoms leaps into sight. The vision across the lake of the snowcapped mountains brings a smile to my lips. I can't believe my luck to be here, this year, this month, and this moment.

Last night's rain left its soft footprints on the earth and its plants. Grateful for the nighttime drink, buds on trees and bushes unfold their gifts this morning. The award of the day goes to the catalpa trees who overnight have thrown open the doors and let their tiny orchid flowers burst forth. I fill my lungs with their fresh fragrance.

I pause before some blue spruce trees and witness their new growth. Last year's blue-green stems are now topped with celery-colored extensions—one inch—and I reach out and caress the silky new growth. Like extended fingernails, they wave in the breeze, enticing, calling me to participate in the newness of life.

I watch a family of ducks quietly cut through the still lake water. A mother and her six baby ducks leisurely proceed, their wake spreading out in a perfect V formation. So confidant are they, so filled with grace and serenity as they glide across the mirror of the water.

I breathe deeply and let go of the minutia, the bombardment of the world. I let go for today the remaining pain from the deaths of those I love. Everywhere I look I see the renewal of God's earth. Why not look within myself for the same.

I realize that the little duck family will eventually be separated; the little ones will grow up and sail off on their own. Perhaps there is danger lurking just ahead, but for right now this mother duck and her six little ones are together and proceeding as if this moment is all there is. And this moment *is* all there is. Would that I could mentally live here in the park with its steady beauty, its confidence in this moment. And I ask myself, "Why not?" Because I allow the concerns and doubts of the world to interfere. I allow my sun to go under the cloud of disbelief too many times, my dreaming to be undermined and stomped upon.

I carry this vision of a secure world in renewal back home. And I am determined to allow this momentary serene space in my mind and heart to exist and grow, regardless of what appears in the next moment.

Bent Limb

I called several tree companies. No one was willing to come out for just one tree, and especially not at a public park. But the single tree with the bent bough that needed pruning was more than just a tree to me. I had planted two crab apple trees, one with pink blossoms, the other with white, in the park by the lake in memory of the two of my children who ended their lives. For three years I watched these trees through harsh winters. I watered their dry roots in the hot summers. On my morning walks in the park, it was comforting to pass the trees and murmur, "I love you."

At one time vandals had torn limbs off the small pink crab apple tree. The tiny angels I hung on the highest limbs of these trees would disappear within days. Not only was I perplexed, but saddened, and then angry about this theft, until a friend suggested that I make the trees "giving trees." So, I put little notes on the next angels I hung. They said, "This is a gift from Lee, a gift from Janis." When they disappeared, I felt better. Perhaps someone needed an angel.

But this summer I noticed a large lower limb on the pink apple tree seriously bent. It almost touched the ground, giving the tree a lopsided appearance. As I walked around the lake each day, this imbalance nagged at me.

To add insult to injury, weeds were growing up around the roots. The drooping limb was substantial enough that I knew my pruning shears wouldn't be adequate. So I began a search to find a tree company that would cut the limb. The search grew futile. No one would come for one limb. Well, at least I could do something about the weeds. I took my gardening tools to the park and got busy.

I was sitting under one of the trees weeding away when a man, cup of coffee in hand, approached me. "What kind of tree is this?" he asked. "A crab apple tree," I answered. I looked up to see a tall, nice looking man perhaps in his 60's, wearing a fishing hat. As I weeded, he sipped his coffee and talked to me about how he'd grown up and raised his own family in this area. He talked about how things had changed with the growth of the city around the park. He told me the lake was where the cows had fed and watered long ago. There'd been a road down the edge of the park that used to be called "lover's lane." He and his brother had hidden in the tall trees and dropped acorns on the cars.

Usually, I wouldn't have been at ease in this situation, not knowing this man, but somehow I wasn't surprised at his presence. Nor was I irritated. I weeded; he talked. He told me about returning from the Korean War to find the population expanding around this park. How the times had changed from gentle to harsh. All the while he spoke he studied the tree's sagging limb. "That ought to be cut off," he said. I looked up, the sun in my eyes, making him an outline.

"I know," I said, "but the tree companies won't touch it."

"I'll be right back," he said and with that he was gone. Almost instantly he was beside me with a large pruning tool. Pointing to where he was going to cut, he waited for my permission. I nodded. The limb came off and the tree right away assumed a more balanced stance.

"I really want to thank you," I said. And for some reason I added, "Actually, it's very important to me that these two trees thrive. I lost two children and I planted these trees in their memory." The man shifted his hat back and said, "I'm so sorry. I lost a son. So I know how that feels." There was a comfortable silence as I continued to weed. I leaned back and took off my gloves and when I looked up, he was gone. I looked at the street and the houses across the street but saw no one.

Our needs are often met in unexpected, surprising ways—angels are what I call these people who appear just at the right moment, offer appropriate help and quietly exit.

Season's Promise

From losses in life one central reality has surfaced: My task is to love life while not trusting that it will remain constant.

On my walks in the park I sit awhile and notice the lazy roll of the creek. It never stops, and I watch as a brown leaf in the creek gets caught in some brush—a time to rest, to gather strength. Eventually I watch the leaf release itself to get back into the flow, rejoin the stream of life. In grief there is a timeout period, a time to be still, and then the time to move on. Observing some backed-up water caught in a dead end, I see that the water is stagnant and gray, with cobwebs on top. There is no inlet and no outlet. The flow has stopped. So it is with the life force when growth and movement are halted.

Fall brings poignant memories of many shared Septembers. Looking at the distant vision of fall's presentation, the Aspen trees turning gold, it appears that God has a giant pail of gold which he tips every September, spilling streams of yellow down crevasses and across mountains. I love to listen to the wind chimes of the aspen leaves, as they rustle against each other, heart shaped leaves with scalloped edges dangling from two-inch stems, freeing themselves to move in the breeze.

Shades of green, bittersweet reds, cinnamon and nutmeg appear on trees and bushes in the fall and bring nostalgia for loved ones so "not there." I watch the leaves die and gently waft downwards to form a brown crunching under my feet.

In winter how stark tree limbs seem without their summer clothes, so vulnerable. But all is not over. The beauty of the tree's life does not end with winter. In spring trees will decorate themselves anew. If the soul of trees lives on, I cannot question the human soul living on. Each season is full of promise for tomorrow.

What Else Could I Have Done?

I watched a movie last night that touched me deeply. It was *Good Will Hunting*[2] about a gentle, compassionate therapist trying to help a disturbed young man.

The young man had highly developed defenses, firmly in place since childhood. His therapist struggled to break through. He persisted in trying to engage the youth and reach deeper. Finally came the scene where the young man admitted that his stepfather had physically and sexually abused him. The therapist moved slowly to face his client. Engaging his eyes, the therapist said, "It's not your fault." The boy shrugged. "It's not your fault," his therapist said again, and the boy said, "Yeah, I know." Closer the therapist came, repeating over and over the same soft statement, "It's not your fault," until what he was saying was heard, really heard. The young man sagged and began crying, reached out and grabbed his therapist, sobbing into his shoulder. That was the breakthrough the therapist had been waiting for. With acknowledgment came acceptance, opening the door to healing.

It's not just children who are victims of this faulty belief system of silence and denial. I thought of the many parents who need to hear, really hear, this simple statement, "It's not your fault," and believe it. Those who bring children into the world and watch something happen to them that the parents could not control but continue to feel responsible for nevertheless.

This hit me hard because of the two children I lost—only in their early thirties—events that shook my world. It has been many years since I lost these children, and still I find myself at times overwhelmed with remorse. The question of what else I could have done to prevent their decisions to take their lives haunts me.

Out in the world going about my day, sometimes the smallest things trigger memories, and the still-raw places in my heart. I know today

---

2.   Ben Affleck and Matt Damon, *Good Will Hunting* (*Miramax Home Entertainment*, 1997)

that these places will always ache, and sometimes it's comforting, when I recall a funny situation or statement, and I feel the gratitude of having had these dear children in my life. But on bad days, I question myself; searching for one more thing I could have done to produce different results in their lives. On some of these difficult days I call Gerald, the therapist who walked me through my children's deaths. Patiently, he tells me the same thing. "It's not your fault. There was *nothing* you could have done to change the path they had to travel."

Riding in the car the other day this question in my mind appeared again. But this time the statement, "It's not your fault," overrode the question.

For some reason, I got it that day. The truth traveled from my intellect down into my heart, and landed in my gut. I got it that there was nothing I could have done to change the outcomes for my children. Nothing. In those days, before medical science had created help for those with brain chemistry complications, the illness shared by my children carried a bleak prognosis that ultimately manifested itself in their deaths. It was as if my son and daughter smiled down at me and reassured me that this was true.

Say it until you believe it, Mom. "It's not your fault."

The Healing Place

I return as often as possible to visit a small section of Texas that remains a balm in my heart—the Texas hill country, green rolling hills, roads that wind beside the Guadalupe River.

Spider webs, silken threads, catch me, rocking me gently in a cradle of pleasant memories of my benign past. Like a treasured old quilt, each section rolls out another happy memory. I visit my beloved Camp Mystic where I spent many summers making treasured friendships. I was nine when I left my house in West Texas to find a whole camp full of friends and activities there. Coming from the arid desert of West Texas, my first sight of the river and the tall cypress trees, whose toes were bathed in the constant flow of the river, filled me with awe. Now, visions of campfires and singing, of swimming in the buoyant river, the slowing down of life's momentum, bring a smile to my lips. This was where I rested and played in perfect safety long ago.

I sit by the river and watch the gentle flow that has always existed. Its permanency is established. The deer bound and armadillos creep at the same pace as before. In this cocoon of timelessness and security, I feel suspended in hope.

This gentle river was where I came much later in life after the death of my son, to soothe and comfort my aching heart. Where I stretched out on a float, eyes closed, and listened to the sounds of the river, the water lapping at the float slowly edging me downstream. Where I slipped into the cool water, and, floating on my back, felt supported, held by invisible hands. The call of birds through the silence opened troubled spots in my soul and the healing energy of river water bathed the pain out of my limbs and mind.

This was where I returned to water my dry eyes, and when the tears came, they washed me clean. I'm home, my body told me. I'm home to heal.

How's Your Husband?

During my early morning walk in the park today, a woman who lives in my building walked toward me. I don't know her well but occasionally we ride the elevator together and I see her walking in the park.

As she approached with a smile she paused and asked, "How is your husband?" Thrown off balance, I replied, "You must have me confused with someone else in our building. I don't have a husband." She apologized (no need, I told her) and we conversationally tried to figure out whom it was she was thinking about.

As I continued on the path around the lake my sense of humor kicked in. I could have said, "I don't know. I haven't seen him in fourteen years." Or, "I haven't checked in with him as yet this morning," or "Wow! He's fantastically happy in his new phase of life," or issued a simple, rather curt, "He's dead."

Hardly anyone I know would appreciate those responses. Too frequently it seems people skid around death, escaping the mere mention. There is an embarrassment, as if one had suddenly confronted something off limits, ugly, and the mystery is unnatural and tainted.

But death is a part of life. For all I know it just might be the "grand finale." In fact, that is precisely how I choose to think of it. Having lost four dearly loved family members, my mother, my husband, a son and a daughter, in the space of six years, I find myself surprised and saddened by the reluctance of our culture to recognize death as a part of life, a natural extension. My personal Christian faith gives me an assurance about death but for so many people that which defies the intellectual knowledge, that which cannot be neatly pigeonholed, seems best left unspoken and unrecognized.

The phenomenon that troubles me the most is the reluctance of others to allow me to talk about those no longer with me. They nod politely and change the subject. If I recall a memory of my loved one no longer here, they slide into discomfort, looking off in the distance or at the ground, until I have finished. How I long for someone who knew my loved ones to ask about my memories of them, to let go of the fear of their own mortality long enough to enter into reminiscence with me.

But what is the source of this discomfort. After all, we know death is a reality. I wonder if the thing they cannot face is my pain. Most people put off the acceptance that life presents us all with death. We will all lose people in our lives that we love. As usual, we cling to that with which we are familiar, the usual, the daily. Fear of death is like a pole set in concrete. To face my pain means they must face their own fear.

Thank you God that you have gifted me with warm-hearted friends and family who *do* allow me my thoughts and memories. I desire to thank those understanding people. Maybe on the other side, there is humor, the ones who have crossed over are laughing at our stumbling responses. As for me, I do not fear the crossing myself. I know I will find those loved ones waiting for me and we'll smile over humanity's ignorance and lack of trust.

The Comforter

I arrived home from work exhausted, down in the dumps. Donning sweats, I climbed onto my bed, and, cradling a pillow in my arms, surfed the television for something to distract my tired mind. My surfing was stopped by a quiet voice that felt like warm oil on my dry and scratchy soul. Quietly, this man talked to his audience in slow, measured, comforting tones. "I want you to know how very important you are," he intoned. "You are special to me. And everyday I look forward to being with you." Fred Rogers of "Mr. Rogers' Neighborhood," the popular television show that ran for so many years, spoke straight into the camera to the children in his unseen audience. He was also talking to me.

I was in the middle of a divorce, submerged in the suffering and conflict that attach to a dying marriage. There is nothing sadder than the demise of a promise, the last breath of the illusion of happiness lasting into old age. My husband and I had lives that severely diverged, and we lost our way in a forest of misunderstanding. What started out as happiness and comfort had twisted into contorted shapes until finally I knew that if I was to survive, I had to go. No lonelier stance existed, but it felt imperative.

So, on those early bleak afternoons when I returned home from work, I would seek relief in Fred Rogers' program. I needed to be talked to as a little girl for I felt terribly frightened and small. To be told in the soft, authentic voice facing the camera, "Your thoughts are important and so are your feelings. I will always be here for you," released my constricted lungs and allowed me deeper breath. The music and the calm, mild-mannered friend who came in, put on his cardigan sweater, sat down, and talked to the camera, soothed me into neutral waters and brought a ray of hope.

I sent Mr. Rogers a letter telling him how he'd helped me, and he replied with a supportive personal letter.

I want to thank you, Mr. Rogers, for your contribution not only to the children who watched, but for all those in need of the safety that you radiated to your audience. For me, it was a time of letting go, the only one in my day. You were an island of protection in a scary world. Out the window went the guilt, the fear, and the anxiety, at least for that hour. I miss you.

The Key On The Tree

One day while surfing the Internet, I saw on a web page, which I did not record, a quote by Albert Einstein, "There are two ways to live your life. One is as though nothing is a miracle. The other is as if everything is a miracle."

A storm raged in the city last night. Sixty mile-an-hour winds drove the rain as it invaded crevices in buildings and made lakes of the streets. The next morning it appeared as if a giant hand had grasped aged trees near the ground, yanked them up, root and all, and threw them across streets and pathways, into houses, and on top of cars.

I took my walk early this morning and observed the massive destruction. Anxiously I hurried down leaf-and-limb strewn paths to the spot where I'd planted the two trees in memory of my children. At the very least I expected to see them battered. To my surprise, they appeared unshaken, standing tall amidst the turmoil around them, as if a cone of protection had surrounded the trees throughout the night.

Something gleamed from a limb of one of the trees. Curious, I walked up to see what it was. It was a single car key on a heart shaped key ring. How did the key get there on a short limb of the tree, about eye level? Could the wind have swept up a lost key from the path and deposited it on the tree limb or had someone placed the key there? It was only 6:30 in the morning. Not many had passed by yet.

I sat down on a nearby bench to take in the vision of the sun coming up to shine on the small lake before me and to think about this item dangling from the tree I'd planted in memory of my son. Then I remembered a similar occurrence two years ago after a sudden violent summer storm. Then, too, I went to check on the trees and found a single, little girl's sandal hanging on the limb of the tree I'd planted in memory of my daughter. I had the same questions about how the little sandal came to be there. I left it hanging and after about a month the shoe disappeared.

As I thought about the trees and the odd things hung on them, I also remembered one day noticing that someone had put a jacket on one of the trees. There it was, a blue denim, light weight jacket hanging from a sturdy limb. I placed the jacket on the grass beneath the tree in case someone returned for it.

I let the images of these objects rest in my mind—interesting items to find on these two trees, so special to me. I sat and mused: suppose my children were giving me some sort of message through these things hanging on the limbs. What did the key, the shoe, and the jacket have in common? Perhaps it was simply, "Keep walking, keep going. Life goes on and you must go with it."

These treasured memorial trees seemed to be gifting me with messages, items appearing as if these were "lost and found" trees. Interesting concept. I struggled mightily without my two children whose capacity to cope with their illnesses had run out so early in their lives. Yet these memorial trees continued to bring thoughts of comfort in unusual visual assurances, and I recognized these symbols as miracles from two precious beings whose spirits would always be with me.

The Flower

"Until the flower is crushed, it cannot make perfume." I saw this on a billboard so I don't know the author. It struck me, however, as a vivid truth about the necessity of an interruption, usually involving the crush of suffering, to bring us to another level of consciousness about life and survival.

In reading about spiritual growth, it seems to be a theory that to grow, to change for the better, we must spend time in the furnace of trouble. I don't know exactly what lessons I am to learn, but I know that I have become more than willing to do anything to escape the furnace in order to learn them. "Just let me know what it is I am to learn, and I promise I will learn it," I say out loud.

But there is good news. In his book, "The Prophet," Kahlil Gibran says, "The deeper that sorrow carves into your being, the more joy you can contain."[3]

This is true for me. The well once brimming with tears I can now fill to capacity with laughter and joy; humor bubbles up from deep inside. I can laugh from the depth of my being, and the biggest laugh comes from watching myself and the bumbling path I sometimes take that circles me back into trouble. Mistakes that used to make me cringe, now elicit a chuckle. "There I go again," I can say, and having called it to consciousness, I am free to change my response.

Have loss and failure and suffering the deaths of my mother, my husband, my son, and my daughter helped me grow stronger? Absolutely. I observe those whose lives have proceeded on an uninterrupted straight line with only small dips and rises on the timeline of their lives. By and large they're content, saying they're the same as they've always been. But to me a flat line defies growth. When I look at a person whose life reads like the stock market—huge ups and downs—I see a person who has usually changed immensely, whose dips in life have produced an expansion into a higher awareness, another level of con-

---

3. Gibran, p. 52.

sciousness. Something new has been born out of the death of some perception, belief system, or old thinking pattern that was smashed with
suffering.

There is a strength and beauty about many of the people who have
faced and endured hardship and grief. Like the crushed flower, a light,
pleasant aroma seems to surround them. There is ease, a flow to their
lives, not present previously. There is a freshness and newness that
could have arrived on the scene only from adversity. The gift of acceptance has apparently sweetened those lives as it has mine.

Signs of Assurance

I know it is June because suddenly, overnight, the Catalpa trees are weighted down with their gifts of fragrant blossoms. I walk early in the morning in our park and smile as I am invaded and surrounded by this beauty—each year it seems to give its testimony that life is good. "I'll be back to tell you this again next summer," is the promise. I pick up some fallen blossoms to examine their perfection in detail. Four scalloped edges surround a deep throat of purple and yellow stripes—tiny little orchids clustered in their home of large green leaves. I gaze from this almost unbearable beauty and stretch my vision to the snow-capped mountains. I, who arrived in Colorado from Texas, remain in silent awe of such beauty. I hope I never recover from this delight.

As I walk, I think again about the dear ones I've lost to death. The beauty of the catalpa tree returning to grace us for two weeks every year seems a testimony that the essence of my loved ones cannot be lost. Again, I smile. In my deepest self I know that what appears to be the end is merely a natural transition, a step back into God's arms, for the spirit cannot be destroyed. And as I look for signs, they appear.

After my second husband died during heart surgery, I sat on our patio wondering how I was to go on. Wiping tears from my cheeks, I glanced at the yellow rose bush we had planted that spring. My husband had called me his "Yellow Rose of Texas." However, this bush we hoped would bear profuse roses that summer had refused to grant us even one. As I gazed at the bush now, I couldn't believe my eyes. Perfects buds were unfolding. I went to examine this miracle and saw that there were six yellow roses—the exact number of years we'd been together.

And quickly, the other deaths—of my mother, then my children—followed, one right after the other. Each and every loss delivered a sign to assure me of the continuing presence of my loved ones, for although they were not where they used to be, they were now to be forever with me wherever I am, in my heart and memories.

After the funeral of my son, I was presented with an astounding sight. I raised my face to look at the sky on this dark, rainy day. I saw on my left black stormy clouds, but on my right, the sky had cleared and a burnt orange and yellow sunset gleamed before me. My son had a particular fondness for sunsets, and this sign assured me, "Do not grieve too long for I am fine."

Some months after my daughter's death, I was visiting the countryside of England with a dear friend. As I gazed at the valley beneath me, a white dove swooped out of nowhere and up to the sky—another sign. The sight of this dove was, for me, another assurance.

So, I am comforted. The central part of each of us—our soul—simply changes form, reverts back to our Maker. The signs assure those of us who are left behind, but who are aware, that all is well, all is well...

Gift Box

I give material gifts to the people I love and also receive them. I realize that I also receive intangible gifts, without bows and decorative paper—gifts of the spirit.

When life presented me with my son's death, I felt as if I'd been handed a black box. I stared long at this heavy, dark thing. It took time but eventually I began to realize I had choices about the box. I could throw it as far as I could and run the other way. I could sit by the black box, cry, and give in to self-pity, which can spread like cancer. I could, by denial, pass the grief to the next person. But the fact remained—I was given this box. It was mine, and I knew it was here to stay.

Day by day I came to accept the heaviness that rested in my hands—the weight of the unexpected, premature death of my son. There was nothing else to do. And with the cessation of struggle came a touch of peace. The whisper turned from, "No, I can't," to, "Maybe I can."

But still the inevitable questions that follow suicides lingered. Why did this happen? How could I have changed things so that it would not have happened? I wrestled with these unanswered questions for some time, wasting energy trying to assign blame. I became tired, bone tired of the heaviness.

Finally I came to realize that such questions would forever remain unanswered. The question—if I had to have one—was not why or how. The question was, *what*. What was I going to do with this black box? What was I willing to do to lift this darkness into light? What next?

Action is affirming and healing. So, I let it be known that I wanted to share my experience with others, and with that willingness arrived many hurting people who turned into good friends. We saw that our experience was in many ways the same. We assured one another we were not going crazy, we were in grief. We learned to talk and talk and talk about our losses to each other until we literally talked our pain to death.

Slowly, bit-by-bit, we found that as we recovered, we could choose colorful ribbons to put around our black boxes to present as gifts to others—the gift of a hand to hold from one who had been there, the gift of being totally present for one another suffering indescribable grief.

Why Go On?

When I watch people go through unbelievable pain and trauma, I wonder what pushes them onward. The capacity for perseverance seems inborn in some humans. I believe there is not one single thing that cannot be used for good, nor any difficult circumstance that cannot be turned in the opposite direction.

I immediately think of Victor Frankel who was held in a German concentration camp for more than a year. He watched people all around him die. He noticed that some of the most starved and emaciated seemed to have steel built into their minds and bodies. They just wouldn't give up.

Father Richard Rohr, in a tape of his series, *The Great Themes of Paul,*[4] says that the ability to go through intense pain depends upon belief that there is meaning in the circumstance. I think that he is saying that there is a basic, underlying, deep meaning in what is transpiring regardless of how it looks.

I believe that somehow we are given the insight to transform black moments if we have a deep well of belief inside, if we do not abandon ourselves to the circumstances.

Victor Frankel believed the last of one's freedoms was the right to choose ones own way. It was his urgent desire and belief that he had something to say that kept the fire of meaning burning. I picture him writing on scraps of paper, old shirts, anything that came into his possession. And when his writing was interrupted, he held the thoughts in his head. He knew that his captors could take everything away from him. The one thing they could not remove was his spirit.

I've learned my inner barometer is the important measure of what comes next. It's not the outward manifestation of a situation that matters, but how calm, hopeful, and still my insides remain.

---

4.   Richard Rohr, O.F.M., *The Great Themes of Paul, Life as Participation*, (Saint Anthony Messenger Press, Cincinnati, Ohio, 2002, series of eight tapes)

I like mental images, pictures. And when I think of my inner self I see a little airplane flying high above the ground. Mostly the little plane flies along peacefully in a blue, blue sky. But at other times, the small craft is surrounded by heavy storm clouds. Inside the cabin, the pilot adjusts her instruments, picks up the microphone, and requests direction and help.

But while she is in the midst of the storm, she is free to choose to trust or to panic. She can observe the rain on the windshield and feel the bucking of the winds from inside the protected surface of the plane, see the lightening strikes, and still she can choose to rely on the stable atmosphere of courage and belief in her skills.

How do people go on after life delivers its blows, after we lose people from our lives? I like a quote by Teresa Savarin, which appeared on a greeting card, "The greatest gift we can give those who have left us is to live fully in their place." That choice is one I make every day. That's how I go on.

Blue Whale

The phone rang early one morning. Intuitively, somehow I knew it was bad news. It was. A neighbor was calling to tell me that a mutual friend had lost her son to suicide.

I immediately called our friend to ask what I could do to help, and she told me she wanted to see me, could I come over the next afternoon.

With soup in hand I arrived. I knew better than to dish out platitudes. How meaningless, for example, to theorize that her son was in a better place, which often comes from well-intentioned friends who cannot possibly understand. I knew from personal experience that her loss was beyond words. Even I, who shared this terrible life experience wasn't sure what I could say to soothe and comfort my hurting friend. No words would talk her into feeling better. A hug and just sitting with her would be the best thing I could do at this time.

We had tea, and she talked. And cried. I offered tissues and held her hand. As she asked the questions these horrendous deaths bring, something came to mind that I shared with her. It was a story from an old television program, "Barney Miller," a popular police sitcom. The storyline offered not only good drama but depicted the gentleness and compassion of the officers. In one episode, an officer had been forced to kill in the line of duty. The magnitude of taking another's life weighed heavily on him and the following day he couldn't function. Barney sent him home.

That night Barney visited his comrade to offer consolation and support. As he was leaving, Barney stopped at the door and asked, "By the way, do you know why the blue whale, which is the largest mammal on earth, has such a tiny throat, only this big?" Barney made a small circle with his thumb and forefinger. The officer said, "No, I don't."

Barney put his hand on his officer's shoulder, "Because, that's just the way it is," he said.

The more I think about that statement, the more I like its simplicity. Even today, years later, I think of it when confronted with incomprehensible tragedy. There is no way to explain it, no way to take away the pain. It's just the way it is.

My friend wiped away unstoppable tears and said, "This is just so awful." I looked her in the eyes and nodded before I enclosed her in my arms. The real comfort, the magic key to complete communication with this friend was in my words, "I *do* understand, because I have been there."

Changing Hats

Throughout life there are different roles we play, different hats we wear. One day out of my orderly world tragedy struck when I lost the first of my two children with mental illness. Life knocked me to the ground. When I stood up once again, my world was altered, rearranged, changed forever. Gone was the comfort of the predictable. All my hats were knocked off.

With longing, I looked back at some of my happy hats of the past: the childhood "Heidi" hat, where life was safe with a kind grandfather of the mountains. And the young wife's mother-knows-best hat, where everything flowed smoothly. Now with this tragedy I yearned for a warm, cozy knit hat to unroll from my head to my toes, to hide and protect me, keep me safe from new painful reality. Like a caterpillar, I would crawl into the cocoon of this hat.

My recovery from severe trauma was slow and erratic. The graph looked like lightening—a zigzag of mood across my once stable sky. I was left with two alternatives: one, to wear the "Denial" hat—immersing myself in activity, ignoring the deep tug of grief; or two, to wear the "Red Hat of Courage," summoning me to brave the necessary solitude into which fear whispers, "Do not stay here. You will sink and never surface again!" Finally, awareness irritated, like a splinter in my finger. To ignore the discomfort was causing the wound to fester and hurt more. I had to overcome my massive fears.

In the loss of a loved one, especially if it's a premature, unexpected death, there is a deep, unspeakable pain. It burns away all the debris, all the trivial. I surrendered to the heartache, allowed myself to stare eye-to-eye at my loss, caress the memories of my child, and let the warm wetness of tears cleanse and begin to heal my heart.

Ultimately, I embraced the pain, sank down to the very bottom of the pool, where I experienced a curious release. It's only by reaching the bottom that we have a surface from which to push off, in order to rise to the top again.

The process through loss and grief snakes its way slowly through the desert. The voyage required time, patience, and fortitude. The caterpillar of grief that seemed so hopelessly ugly and unproductive, finally one day began to open, to lessen its hold on hardness. As the wonder of the butterfly emerges, it is at first vulnerable and hesitant. Then as its wings dry and strengthen, it unfolds in glorious beauty, and the butterfly boldly takes on its new life. The butterfly cannot decide to reverse and return to the caterpillar even if it wants to.

So it is with grief, with the countless losses throughout life. Small letting go's, to huge releases. I cannot go back now. The letting go of old hats and roles that seemed so frightening turned out to be freedom. I moved from reliance on my outer world to reliance on my inner world. The strength I found was not my own. It belonged to God, to his son whose intense suffering ended in the glory of resurrection. Sought after, longed for, pleaded for, my faith was rewarded with a strength and courage I knew that I, by myself, did not possess. An invisible hand upheld me.

Like wearing a "First Officer" hat in the airplane preparing for take off to this new life, I could hesitate, and decide to remain on ground, rejecting the unknown possibilities of flight. I could close my eyes, refuse to change, to stretch through the pain and grow. Or, I could accept the challenge and thrust the lever into full speed. Now there would be no stopping the acceleration. It's a GO. There is no hesitation now, no turning back. Straining mightily, the airplane will lift from the ground and swiftly, easily take flight.

My soul abandoned itself, relaxed into the benign powers that be, surrendered to what is, and to God. Going with, not resisting, I quit fighting. The letting go, the release of old hats, old roles, offered me a beautiful, if scary world, and a brand new freedom.

So, what about those old hats I wore? Like Mary Tyler Moore in her popular television series, *The Mary Tyler Moore Show*,[5] I could throw my old hats high into the sky. Throw them up with a smile. My new

---

5.   James Brooks and Allen Burns, *The Mary Tyler Moore Show*, CBS, 1970-1977.

hat is constructed with patches of all my old hats, for these roles were part of me and always will be. My mosaic-patterned hat need not be compared to another. And I am free to add to this comfortable hat I now wear. It's aged and wise and offers serenity unknown to me before.

Waves

I loved going to the beach when I was a child. Living in dry, land-locked El Paso, a trip to the ocean was a treat. For several summers, my best friend and I traveled to Santa Monica Beach in California with our parents. At the beach, we would stand at the tide's edge waiting for the waves. As the swells approached, we'd turn and run as fast as we could. We escaped time after time the experience and the risk of being engulfed by the sea.

There came a time, urged on by my big brother, when I was ready to walk into the incoming waves, when I decided to go forward to meet them. That day I turned and faced the waves and let them break over me. They threw me off balance. I staggered, but recovered, thrilled. I ventured out further. The further I went, the easier it became. The strength of the breaking waves no longer hit me with full force. Soon I rose with the waves, involuntarily lifted by the swell. Overcoming the fear was exhilarating.

Later on I saw a metaphor for life in this childhood game with the sea because the time came when it was necessary to turn and face the waves of life instead of running from them. I felt the inescapable need to risk, to force myself beyond my comfort level. I felt the push to stand up and move forward, to surmount.

In my early forties, my vague sense of longing crystallized into knowledge that I was yearning to choose a path of my own in the search for my spiritual self. It meant releasing the bland, carbon copy ideal of my young-adult years. It meant trusting myself at long last, and choosing to believe in a God whose ways I did not have to figure out, letting go of the need for logical explanations and fixed answers.

When life presented the deaths of the four major anchors in my family, I thought of that first time when I turned and faced the sea, of the choice presented. I could turn and run, dodge the trauma. Or I could turn and walk straight into the pain. I did the thing that I most did not want to do. The only way for me out of this excruciating grief was to walk through it. Not away from it, nor around, above, or underneath it, but straight through to the other side. I walked steadily into the inevitable, rolling swells of the waves and was raised automatically above them.

I quit fighting my reality. Somehow instinctively I knew that the resistance to the pain was causing more pain. The more I protested inwardly, the worse I felt. The rhythm of the waves of life seems to chant, "Go with it," and, "Trust, trust."

While life's blows will always hurt, I can survive. And for my lost loved ones, they're now safely with me wherever I am, even as I walk into the waves of life.

The Passing

It is July 21, 1999, and this morning will be the burial at sea of John. F. Kennedy, Jr., his wife Carolyn, and her sister, Lauren—tragic victims of a plane crash.

The violent deaths of these young people, so full of promise, confront me again with the loss of my own beautiful grown children within three years of each other.

Taking a walk in the park early this morning, I pass a lovely sight. Fragile impatiens petals in pink, purple, coral, lavender, and white form a dancing ring around the base of an oak tree. The sun is just appearing, and the light peaks over a roof and shines on half of the bed of flowers. When I return an hour later, the other side is also in the sunlight.

When I confront the concrete fact of death, the sight of these vulnerable, brief flowers reminds me how fleeting life is. If the world were concentrated right here in this flower bed around this tree, if we humans were the ring of flowers and the sun was life, the first rays would light only a small section at our birth. Then the light would spread, widened by the imperceptible march of time until finally the whole bed of our humanity would be flooded with sunlight.

These tiny points of color, these flowers, only exist in the summer. By late fall they will fade and disappear. They are present to our sight in earth's timetable for such a short time. We try to capture their brilliance in photographs, to make this beauty last.

I would like so much to fix them forever, as they are, in full bloom, like anchoring my comforts, my securities, my loved ones firmly to me. I don't want to lose this, let this sight change into anything new and different. I want it to stay as it is. But it won't. It can't. At any rate, by nightfall the vision will be gone, in darkness. But just because I cannot see the flowers does not mean they are not there. And in winter, they remain in my thoughts, in my memories.

Just the fact that this lovely sight *did* exist, these children *did* exist, and I was fortunate enough to participate in their beauty has to be enough. The flowers and my precious offspring never promised to stay. I try to internalize the beauty, the goodness, the purity, and make it a part of me. In that way I can keep the vision of the flowers; in that way my lost loved ones remain a part of me forever. But for the struggle to grow through the grief, I would not have experienced this beauty.

Desert Gift

An airplane trip to Phoenix right before Mother's Day propelled me into sadness. I hadn't visited Phoenix since my daughter took her life five years prior after spending years in Phoenix trying to gain a sense of well being. She'd be fine for a time. She attended college for a short period and seemed all right, but then the familiar weight of depression would again descend. She courageously bore the heaviness of her illness for years. I had asked God many times to show me that Janis was now at peace and would feel I'd received an answer, but then I would ask again, because I'd need to be reassured repeatedly.

The plane bounced over the mountains of Colorado and Utah. Cloud cover prevented the sight of these stunning peaks, so I leaned back in my seat and closed my eyes. The old heartache and heaviness engulfed me. And then, just as quickly, came this new thought: "*No. Lightness now.*" It was as if Janis was whispering in my ear, "No more heaviness, Mom. I am all right. Carry me in lightness now. Feel the lightness." The words stayed with me as I descended from the plane and deeply inhaled the desert air. I grew up in the Southwest and have always felt a compelling spiritual pull in the desert. It's a place of sunshine and healing which was a major reason why I picked Arizona as the best location for Janis. The mental health system was the best I could find, and the doctors and others who worked with Janis and me were compassionate, helpful, and loving, always going the extra mile. There was also an inner urge that told me this was the restoring place for Janis. I remember asking my daughter if she knew the myth of the Phoenix who perishes in flames and then is born anew—a renewal, recycling, a letting go of the old to rise up again better than ever. The flight of the Phoenix represents the capacity to leave the world and its problems behind, fly towards the sun in pure, clear skies. It is a symbol of immortality and spiritual rebirth. When I told Janis the story she smiled. She had not heard it before.

The friend I was visiting took me to Sedona where a preview of the Grand Canyon greeted us. Centuries of wind and water sliced through the mountains leaving cliffs of red and purple striations and temples of rock displaying the work of God's majestic creativity. High above the little town was a flat mesa that served as the Sedona airport. I watched with mounting excitement as a small plane raced down the limited space, just in time lifting into the blue sky with freedom, the weighty metal instantly transformed into weightlessness. As I stood and watched, lightness edged into me, elbowing the heaviness, claiming space and lightening the burden I had clutched so tightly for years.

The next day I walked with my friend to the mall to pick up a package he'd ordered. My daughter wasn't physically present anymore, not here, not anywhere, yet in Phoenix I felt her presence all around. I sat on a bench waiting while he went inside the store. Directly in front of me was the small window of a shop filled with angels. In the center of the window display was a large alabaster angel with her arms stretched upward. I smiled as I gazed at the light radiating through the milky glass behind the statue. My breath seemed to have more room to move through my insides. My friend came out of the store with his package and we walked back down the mall. I paused, as I usually do, at an outside counter bearing samples of perfume and lotion and sprayed a scent on my wrist. It was fresh and delicate. I looked at the bottle. The name of the scent was Angel Breath. I smiled.

On the last day of my visit, we went to the Phoenix Art Museum to see the works of Dale Chihuly, a renowned glass artist. Tables, and walls, and one ceiling were filled with free forms of glass, shapes of color, each design more breathtaking. The rooms were dark with a spotlight on each piece, the light appearing to emerge and flood upwards from beneath each piece. My daughter's silent message received on the plane echoed, "No more darkness. Lightness now, Mom." Here the mix of peaceful, quiet works and audacious dramatic pieces seemed to shout, "Here! Look at this!" It was a radiant assault on the senses, light reflecting and glittering through each object in darkened rooms.

To create these pieces, from searing heat, rigid glass is released from its limitations, permitting fluid movement, freeing swirls of color to merge and blend. From the crucible of fire emerges great beauty, possible only through extreme heat. Likewise, from the crucible of fire the Phoenix arises.

Giant chandeliers hung with four hundred individual pieces of glass, the light shining through each piece piercing the darkness. The exhibit walk led its visitors through a narrow room with a glass ceiling. I looked up to see hundreds of forms; light reflecting through shapes of brilliant blues and reds, clear greens and yellows. There was a sense of no boundaries, exactly as the brochure stated, "Liberated glass exploding from restriction." Buttered yellows and ember reds enfolded me; deep sea greens and blues washed me in waves. My senses were flooded with awe, with relief and joy. I felt released from my tight little world, knots of concerns, material things and endless minutia. Inside, suddenly, I felt catapulted into another dimension of endless possibilities, breathless hope. I felt a swoop of joyous energy. It was Einstein who said, "When we unlock the mystery of light, we will find God."

It was not until later when I looked at the address of the museum that I noticed the street was the same street on which my daughter's life had ended. Again, my heart connected with my awareness of the significant vibes of comfort I felt my daughter was sending me.

I left Phoenix with a deep healing. The gifts that I was open to receive were lightness, grace, and joy. I felt profoundly comforted and could now trust that—regardless of the raw facts—all was well.

Reports occasionally surface about someone finding a large bank account they'd not been aware of, a gift just waiting to be discovered and used. I received just such a gift with a deep well of blessings that surprised me with its bottomless bounty. That treasure was the presence of God in my life.

8

Eyes of Faith

Stretcher from Heaven

For most of my life I believed that knowledge was all I needed. Higher education staunchly indoctrinated that life would be much better if academically prepared.

While knowledge definitely has its place, it was life that led me to uncover and value what lies deeper, beyond the words of scholars. Beneath pure information lies a deep well of pivotal resources that I did not tap until forced to do so through adversity. For a baby chicken to live, the shell has to crack open. Apparently for me also there must be a splitting, often painful, to reveal the treasure within.

The beginning of a favorite poem of mine by Rumi, "Zero Circle," states:

> Be helpless, dumbfounded,
> Unable to say yes or no.
> Then a stretcher will come from grace
> To gather us up.

Later in the poem, Rumi goes on to say:

> We are too dull-eyed to see that beauty
> If we say we can, we're lying.
> If we say No, we don't see it,
> That No will behead us
> And shut tight our window onto spirit.

I believe the author is telling me that to truly find God and discover his grace, I have to be rendered helpless, dumbfounded. The Twelve-Step programs know this. In fact, they offer that only in a state of surrender can we be rescued, freed from the bondage of addiction. No moral psychology or adherence to rules ever kept an addict from his agony.

The last of Rumi's poem states:

> So, let us rather not be sure of anything
> Besides ourselves, and only that, so
> Miraculous beings come running to help,
> Crazed, lying in a zero circle, mute,
> We shall be saying finally,
> With tremendous eloquence, Lead us.
> When we have totally surrendered to that beauty,
> We shall be a mighty kindness.

No matter how strictly I follow the rules, keep up the appearance of worthiness, follow society's dictates, often I can't find that worthiness until I fail. When the academic lessons ring hollow, the rules suddenly seem ludicrous. Finally I find that for me worthiness is not found on the outside, in the world that measures and judges. It seems that only in my despairing moments can I admit that by myself alone I cannot find peace, within or without.

Once I can say without reservations, "I don't have the answers," that formal education has failed me in finding inner peace, then and only then am I "gathered up by a stretcher from grace." Then, magically, as I am propelled into willingness to ask for help, relief comes as knowledge that no matter how grim the circumstances surrounding me, deep down all is well. I cannot know the future outcome and that fact is okay.

Believing Is Seeing

"I have to see it to believe it," goes the old saying. Now I am finding that the reverse is true, at least for me. By believing, I finally see.

In my youth, I reserved judgment until I had visual proof. Turning this around, I asked myself, "What if I have a strong belief and then look for validation?"

In mid-life, when crisis after crisis slammed me, I found that I had to choose either to believe in God's mercy and love, or live out the rest of my life in bitterness. Blame God for life's blows and tragic losses, or accept that bad things happen in life, and that God had always been there to support me through grief. To accept that he is not the judging, punishing God of the past, but a very real presence of good, of compassion, and forgiveness.

But arriving at this destination required a bit more suffering than I anticipated. The world had been telling me since childhood that money and prestige were what mattered, if one follows all the rules success follows. But "success" didn't bring the sense of belonging I expected. It didn't bring serenity or peace of mind. All I knew was that deep down there was a blank space in my soul. And this hole that I tried to fill with society's values only became deeper with time. No amount of denial, no amount of running away, or overindulgence eased the pain.

I careened into brick walls with the rules and values to which I'd long attached myself. They simply were not adequate to alleviate the pain of change and loss. I couldn't follow my old road map. Life presented, rather *forced*, the final choice. My alternatives were to believe in God, trust in him with all my heart, or to turn my back on him. To rage in anger at God for taking my loved ones, or to realize that he had not "taken" them—he had received them. I chose to believe the latter.

This time it was not an intellectual practice, not a set of new rules to follow, but surrender, a heartfelt acceptance of my dependence on a higher being, a trust in the underlying structures of mercy that I cannot see. And so, coming to believe and longing to trust, I set out deliberately to find God's abiding love every day. I look for it in the ordinary, in the least likely people and places. Surprised and delighted, finally I see, because I believe.

Glasses

At one time in my life I thought it too risky to trust, too full of unknowns, to believe that a benevolent higher being or anything other than myself, could be in charge of my life. I preferred to stay in the illusion of total control—that I managed just fine. Plus, I was familiar with the discomfort plaguing me at that point in my life. So, I'll stay here, tolerating my misery, trusting my own guidance, because at least I know what to expect, I told myself, and knowing what to expect equaled safety.

For a long time I believed that. But one day it became painfully clear that this way of life didn't work anymore. Earthquakes appeared along the fault line, shaking me loose from the rigidity of old ways.

It was like going out to lunch with friends and discovering I could not read the menu with my old glasses. Despite efforts to clean and adjust them, they were useless. The world was no longer easily navigated receiving it through my old glasses. Thus it was with old habits and ways.

In retrospect, they no longer functioned as a compass to lead me to paths of rightness and comfort. I believe it was the rapid loss of my loved ones that pushed me to walk through another door, to reach out and find something that pulled me out of the dark into light, into seeing life with a different focus.

Life is like entering an optical company at birth. Everybody receives glasses designed specifically for him or her. In our boxes, which have our names on them, we'll find glasses that will reveal the pain of growing up, of loss, of defeat. These glasses will also present us with pleasures and successes. However much we dislike the glasses handed us, there is nothing to do but accept them.

But there is a second door in this optical company, less visible, which is available later on in life, if we look for it, dare to open it. This door leads to an exchange department and this time we get to choose. Not everyone elects to enter the second door to exchange his or her glasses. Some prefer to exist with the old familiar ones even though their vision remains limited.

I selected the second door and found that my new pair of glasses revealed God in all situations, and this vision altered my life. As Father Richard Rohr says, "God is always present in every transforming moment whereby we can choose again, whereby we can surrender again, whereby we can say yes again."

With simple trust I reached out for a replacement for the old, and my view became clear. Old ideas and judgments disappeared like sun clearing the fog. How freeing the experience of seeing the world in a different light. And the question became, "How can I use these new glasses to help others, to make good come from whatever life hands me?" Alone, by myself, my vision is half-strength. With God's help my vision can become 20/20.

Merging Images of God, Self, and the World

After listening to tapes by Father Richard Rohr while I walk the park, I often find myself writing my own thoughts. This morning Father Rohr explained that there are three images we all have that govern our lives: image of self, of the world, and of God. When one of these images changes, the others follow suit.

Running the mental video of my life for self-image, I see a shy, overly sensitive child growing into a young woman steeped in denial; an everything-is-fine adult; and finally, through life's twists and trage-dies, an image of me walking through dark clouds emerging as a strong, capable, loving woman.

My image of the world began with perceiving the world to be safe, just, and right. That image changed to one of a world consumed by confusion and fear. But it wasn't until my image of God changed that it was possible for my self-image and my worldview to be altered.

My childhood image of God was of a loving, but somewhat intimi-dating and distant entity somewhere up in the sky. There came a time in midlife that this smoky image turned into one of confusion and anx-iety. But this hurt so much that eventually I decided I could not stay there, that I had to make a choice: either a benevolent, personal God exists or He doesn't. It seemed that bare bones simple. I could shut the door on God and live out the rest of my life with questions and half-beliefs, or I could fling open the doors to my mind and heart, trusting God with everything. After some struggle, I chose the latter. It was like choosing life over death.

The cloak of my old theories ripped and fell away, leaving me exposed and vulnerable, but available. Slowly I began a daily search for God's presence in my life and in my world, not so much in a sacred or exalted place, a formal, structured environment, but in the everyday, the ordinary, minute-to-minute existence of my life. In this trusting and looking for God, to my surprise, I found a truer understanding of myself, of the world, and of other people—a secure triangle. My com-passion seemed to widen and deepen, for others and for myself. The closer I felt to God, the empathy and mercy I felt for others seemed to deepen and widen, like a narrow river opening to enter the sea. The three images merged and became more balanced.

Father in the Park

A young man was walking his dog and pushing a baby stroller in the park this morning. As I approached them, the black lab zigzagged back and forth on the path. The baby was crying. The man stopped, reined in the dog, and came around to face his crying child. Kneeling down, he smiled and talked to his daughter.

As soon as she saw the familiar face of her daddy, she stopped crying, her eyes lit up, and a dazzling smile appeared. She was reassured that she was not just bumping along the park path alone.

I could identify with the frightened child. I've often felt as if I were being moved down the road of life too fast by something I could not see and did not trust. As if some mysterious force was maneuvering me, like it or not.

At times when I am overwhelmed, I feel a strong need for the world to stop. Just stop for a while and let me get my bearings. It's like when a season changes abruptly from summer to winter and I am confused. Some events shake my very foundation, but no timeout is granted. The world keeps going, people continue with their lives; business as usual relentlessly inches us forward.

The face of the child lighting up at the sight of her father brought to mind the connection that comes with my awareness of the presence of my God. When I have felt alone, been pushed along on the path of life with no visible instigator, I am afraid. Remembering the presence of God, with me all of the time, relieves my panic and restores trust. There is guidance—if I am aware of my need and seek it. The necessary attitude is one of hope and trust; and most of all, I must ask for assurance. The baby in the carriage had to let her father know by crying that she needed to know he was near. In that way, she asked for his reassurance. And she received it. Her father appeared in front of her with a smile.

There will be another time when that child will want to know she is not alone. So also with most of us. In my need I make a request of God, asking to be aware of his presence. I open up to the possibility that he is there, and my simple willingness gives me the assurance, the affirmation I need, time after time, day after day.

Struck By God

How surprising to be struck by God's grace, granted amnesty and mercy, accepted right where I am in life. Some people don't believe this exists. It's too good to be true. The feeling of unworthiness abounds. All of us can decide we're not worthy of God's love and abundance, that this thing we did or did not do will interfere with unconditional grace. We just don't deserve it. This message from Father Richard Rohr's tape in the series, "Great Themes of Paul," suggests that this is what most of us believe—that we don't deserve this grace.

I believe that all of us deserve a pardon from God. Father Rohr says: "God deals with human unworthiness by a pre-emptive mercy strike. It's a given, our unworthiness. A given for all humankind. God does not love us *if* we change. God loves us so that we *can* change."

Recently I visited the Grand Canyon for the first time. As I gazed at the depth, the width and color of this awesome beauty I thought, "This is what it's like to be struck by God. Fully accepting God's love for me looks and feels like this."

But how many of us really believe this? Many strive for A's, to be placed on a religious honor roll by good deeds. But God places no emphasis on competition. In fact, it probably appears on his "do not do" list. There is a difference between those who desire to serve God and do so with just that in mind, and those who desire to be seen serving God.

I personally just love the saying, whose author I do not know: "Sitting in church does not make you a spiritual person anymore than standing in a garage makes you a car." I know a devout man who goes quietly about tending to the needs of the old and infirm. He makes no big announcement of his mercy errands; he merely sees a need and he and his wife quietly take care of it. His kindness to his fellow man, his nonjudgmental attitude towards all radiates the love of God. What a wonderful state to strive for—the state of non-judgment of others. That seems to me to be a key, the sign that we have indeed accepted and believe in God's innate and forever mercy and love for all his creatures.

The love of God can only be experienced within. I have been blessed with that warmth more than once in my own life. After the devastating loss of loved ones, I've knelt and asked for comfort, and there has never been a time when I've not felt an answer to this prayer. I've even voiced the need for a hug from God and then waited. Believing that I will receive it, I am quiet and receptive. Soon enough, a feeling of warmth settles over my being. When I've asked for direction and believe I will receive it, I'm amazed at the way this direction appears, the different messengers God sends.

With so much violence in the world, so much judgment and punishment from one human being against another, it brings me relief and a sense of peace to know that God stands firm—and forever—in his mercy and love for all human beings. I rest better with this belief.

Free From Me

Father Richard Rohr says in his tape, *Letting Go: A Spirituality of Subtraction,* "the only way we can be free from our fears is to be free from ourselves. There is a complete mathematical relation between the amount of fear in people's lives and the extent to which they are attached to themselves."[1]

At times I am not even aware of the silent, pervasive power of fear that sneaks up and clouds my thoughts. All I know is that somewhere inside me there's a discomfort, like a shadowy figure that walks across the back stage of a play. It has no lines to speak, no purpose, but its presence is disruptive.

Relationships are a prominent cause of fears. Perhaps I will lose someone's esteem, or fail to obtain someone's love, or a loved one may be on a path that scares me. At times I finger problems like a Catholic fingers his rosary. Father Rohr says the core of fear, as well as the core of evil, is the ego's need to look good, to control, to be right, be first and be important. He adds that until that need for importance is dealt with in the light of God's help, it blinds us to everything because we don't really meet anyone else. We see everything through our own hurts, fears, desires, and needs. We endlessly meet ourselves in different forms.

How much I desire at times to take a vacation from myself. Perhaps that's the reason people move from place to place, thinking, "If I put my body in another setting I'll be happy. If only I lived over there." But the "over there" eventually becomes "the here" that I wanted to escape in the first place.

Ego lies hidden in a secluded space, inside the human brain, presenting itself as good. We're not aware that it's working to destroy peace of mind. The slogan of ego seems to be, "What's in it for me?" This manipulator—ego—works with strength and energy under-

---

1.   Rohr, *Letting Go: A Spirituality of Subtraction*

ground, not in our consciousness until and unless we are forced into new patterns of thinking, challenging the business-as-usual ego force.

I hope I can serve as a sentry—armed with the flashlight of awareness—of the ego that can erode my life. And I thank you, Father Rohr, for this lesson.

Example

In a lecture I heard a quote from Henry Miller, which stayed within me: "Example moves the world more than doctrine."

When I walk in the park early in the morning, I see an astounding sight. Two men are running together, a short length of rope connecting their wrists. As they approach, I see that one man holds his head up as if he were looking at the sky. His eyes are open and sightless. The other man is purposefully watchful, guiding his friend around potholes and objects.

These men are not merely walking fast. They are running with purpose and a goal in mind. With my eyes, I see the men. With my heart, I see the trust. The genuine trust the blind man grants his friend to guide him is magnificent to observe. No hesitancy, no faltering, no control of speed. They run full stride, all out, fearlessly.

In our world today such trust in anything is rare. We seem increasingly self-focused. Many plunge ahead as if their path is the only one, oblivious of other paths, oblivious to the benches along the way that offer rest. Few stop long enough to be aware of a possible need for change of direction.

At times I, fully sighted and in possession of other faculties, get lost in my walk through life. It takes a chasm appearing before me to compel me to stop, rest, take stock, and search for direction. I don't seem to be able to always *see* which is the right path. That is the time I need to look for a higher source. When I trust him to know, to give me the intuitive nudge towards the right path, when I ask for this, I always receive it.

It is that simple. I ask. Sit awhile and then proceed, trusting in God to have that thin rope around my wrist, like the men in the park, guiding me, showing me the way.

Some days all I need to do is take a walk in the park.

God in a Car Wash

Into my busy morning I was confronted with yet one more thing that I needed to do—get my car washed.

I was feeling harried and hurried, and concerns about different family members and friends held me in a worry box. My body ached; arthritis had chosen today to flare up. *Well just do the next thing*, my mind counseled me. So, I headed for the car wash. I sat in a long line waiting my turn, and my thoughts continued to fret over this and that, like a dog worrying over his bone.

Finally my turn came, I punched in the code, and drove my car into the garage, windows up, radio off. Soon the wand of water hit my car with a blast. Then there followed a showering of soap blocking my view. Once again the blast of water shook my car, cleaning off the dirt. And then the forced air buffeted my car to dry it.

While I sat there, a comforting thought arrived: I will stay dry and comfortable during this whole process. Although the blast of water shakes my car, I am protected inside. When the soap flows overhead and all around, it does not touch me. I stay comfortable and shielded from the blast of air.

And is this not just like God's daily protection? If I will give God permission to do that which he is perfectly capable and willing to do, he will shield me from worry and concern, from the world's craziness. God will place a bubble around me, protecting me from the blasts of daily life. If I will be aware, I can remain in God's protection every day if I but ask for it.

Knowing

The dictionary definition of the word "know" is: "to perceive directly; to recognize the nature of; to be acquainted or familiar with." It is easy to have knowledge of factual material, to receive information about things, people, and places.

Real knowing, though, has come to me when an experience drops its lesson down deep inside. And once I experience a truth, I can't *not* know it. It's like a door, previously closed, opens and now stays open.

As I matured, notions I'd held since childhood had to be expelled from the old belief basket. Previously held views widened to a new vista. This is supposed to happen; it's called growth. But how hard it is to give up once-cherished ideas. For example, the idea that the world would always be safe, that I would remain distant from misery and ill fortune had to be replaced with the reality that life holds mystery and uncertainty, and yes, a well of suffering.

To accept the fact that there is no certainty in life is troublesome. I wonder if the old existential enigma of what life is and where I fit in eventually comes to most of us.

The uncertainty and fragility of life produced fear in me until I realized that I did not have to do this job alone. Eventually, I faced the very real need to trust in something out there other than another human being because humans leave, move away, or die. I'd always believed in God, a benevolent force to whom I could turn. But the idea of God remained a fuzzy ideal until I was forced into full surrender and acceptance by the misery of my efforts to bury problems and disappointments. I had no recourse except to reach out for that power.

Making that decision was a preliminary step. The next steps were to release fear then trust in that power. Once I discovered that underlying hands were supporting me and always would be it was an experience that stayed. I knew. And now knowing, I can no longer *not* know.

Trust—A Step Up from Belief

There is belief and there is trust. I've always believed in God, but evidently have not always trusted him. How many times I pray with an exact image in my mind. "This situation should look like this, don't you know." I especially have a preconceived notion of how relationships should look.

I say I believe, yet insist upon drawing *the* picture for a listening God. Then I'm surprised and disappointed when life does not duplicate my picture. Hours have been spent in diagnosing and prescribing, dictating what my Ultimate Power can and will do.

In my early parenting days I had four children in three different schools, a natural drawback to spacing my children so widely. I carpooled to all these schools, most of the time on busy freeway systems. I was always a bit nervous when entering peak traffic on these speedways. Turning my head, looking behind me, all around me, and having learned not to dally when entering the ramp, I would make a run for it and speedily enter. One day a little voice from the back seat said calmly, "Mrs. Jones, why don't you use your rear view mirrors. Isn't that what they're for?"

Bless little hearts…the wisdom of children. I realized with a start that of course I could depend upon these automobile aids. But when I did not trust enough to use them, of course they did not work. I had not trusted that those mirrors would reveal to me exactly where the surrounding cars were at the time. And wasn't that very much like God? God is always there, just like the rear view mirrors. He's like that. He's never on vacation. If I feel an absence, it is I who am unaware. It is I who does not trust.

I am doing an exciting experiment. In my prayers I tell God that I give him my life and my relationships with family and friends, because I know he wants only good. He is not a punishing God, of that I am sure. I need not dread his will. I am sure his will for my life is in my best interest. I tell him that I recognize that the picture I hold in my head is my own creation. And I am confident that he does know exactly what my life should look like. And I trust him to arrange these wonders all by himself, because I do not know most of the time what is best for me.

I lay down my pre-arranged pictures, and expectations. Then I wait. Sometimes I have to wait awhile. But if I persevere and resist the temptation to paint this picture by myself, lo and behold, sure enough, things rearrange themselves in an amazing way, always surprisingly simple, and the result is something I would never have dreamed of, far better than I could have planned, and in the best interest for all concerned. Like a weak muscle, which is exercised, my trust is strengthened each time. I'm learning to trust as well as believe.

God's Scrapbook

Suppose God has a scrapbook. In it he has his family pictures. God's scrapbook covers many volumes because we are all in it. And we are assured balance in his treatment of us in this journal.

I have ideas about my picture and what it looks like in the record of humanity. I know who should be in the picture with me and exactly what they should look like. This is my life, after all. I turn pages and think I can anticipate the progression for myself and these other people in it.

Then a storm rages, blowing pages out of order. More than one person is no longer in the picture. And another has changed direction, or donned different clothes. This can't be right, I exclaim. Why does it look like this?

My discomfort often comes from the inflexible mental picture I have. I want to show God my vision, and what these other people should be doing so that they fit into my life as planned. I have chosen the design and the colors—but I am frustrated when my vision isn't what I now see before me.

Maybe God wants me to leave the picture up to him—to trust him enough to do this—a stretch of faith, as my friend Judith says. Can I stop fighting to have things my way? Can I let go enough to permit the pruning needed to help me grow? Maybe God wants me to accept that my life will be like a kaleidoscope—changing constantly. The colors are no less bright, no less beautiful. They are ever changing, evolving, perhaps more splendid than my private image. It is possible that God's family portrait is far lovelier than I can envision, if I will permit him to arrange all of us in the scrapbook according to his plan.

And so it is. My journey will continue to change, to branch off into new paths, to lead me on. There will be many doors through which I may walk, many new experiences I may attempt to describe. And this I know, these steps propelling me forward through an open door, these footprints are the most important legacy that I can leave my loved ones. Keep moving. Keep trusting. This is *not* all there is. Just around the corner there is something of magnificence.

THE END

Bibliography

Affleck, Ben, and Matt Damon. *Good Will Hunting.* Miramax Home Entertainment, 1997.

Beattie, Melody. *Codependent No More.* Center City, Minnesota, Harper Collins Publishers, 1987.

Brooks, James, and Allen Burns. *The Mary Tyler Moore Show.* CBS, 1970-1977.

Kaufman, Charles. *Adaptation.* Columbine Tri-Star, 2003.

Dass, Ram. *Conscious Aging.* Boulder, Colorado, Sounds True Recordings, 1992.

Dayson, Susanna. *Girl Interrupted.* New York, Vintage Books, 1993.

Dion, Celine. *Because You Loved Me.* Sony Music Entertainment, [Canada] Inc., 1996.

Gibran, Kahlil. *The Prophet.* New York, Alfred A. Knopf, Inc, 1923.

Housden, Roger. *Ten Poems to Change Your Life.* New York, Harmony Books, 2001.

Oliver, Mary. *The Journey* from *Dream Work.* Grove Atlantic, Inc. New York, 1986

Rohr, Richard, O.F.M. *Great Themes of Paul, Life as Participation.* Cincinnati, Ohio, Saint Anthony Messenger Press, 2002.

Rohr, Richard, O.F.M. *Great Themes of Scripture.* Saint Anthony Messenger Press, 1999.

Rohr, Richard, O.F.M. *Letting Go: A Spirituality of Subtraction.* Cincinnati, Ohio, Saint Anthony Messenger Press, 1987.

Rohr, Richard, O.F.M. *Sermon on the Mount: Awakening of the Heart.* Cincinnati, Ohio, Saint Anthony Messenger Press, 1992.

About the Author

Patricia Forbes was born and reared in El Paso, Texas. Her family moved to Houston where she married and reared four children. Patricia attended Mt. Vernon College in Washington, D. D., University of Houston, and the University of Texas. She received a Bachelor of Science degree in Education. In later years she moved back to her beloved mountain and now resides in Denver, Co.

She wrote and published numerous articles and stories in journals and magazines. One of her articles appeared as the feature story in the *Nami Advocate*, and *The National Voice on Mental Illness* in 2002. Her short story appeared in *Chocolate For a Woman's Soul* in 1997 and another story was published in *Chicken Soup for the Couple's Soul* in 1999.

Patricia has been a regular facilitator of a creative writing class for VIVA, a University of Denver program associated with the Institute of Learning in Retirement. She enjoys teaching memoir writing class, and writing about the beautiful Rocky mountains which embrace the city of Denver.

0-595-32870-9

Printed in the United States
23962LVS00002B/19